DATTATREYA'S

SONG OF THE AVADHUT

Sri Garib Das Oriental Series No. 255

DATTATREYA'S SONG OF THE AVADHUT

An English Translation

Of The Avadhut Gita

(With Sanskrit Transliteration)

—A Classics of Mystical Literature book—

S. Abhayananda

Sri Satguru Publications
A Division of
Indian Books Centre
Delhi, India

Published by
Sri Satguru Publications,
Indological and Oriental Publishers
A Division of
Indian Books Centre
40/5, Shakti Nagar,
Delhi-110007
India

Email: ibcindia@vsnl.com
Website: http://www.indianbookscentre.com

First Indian Edition; Delhi, 2000

ISBN 81-7030-675-2

Published by Sunil Gupta for Sri Satguru Publications, a division of Indian Books Centre, 40/5, Shakti Nagar, Delhi-110007, India and printed at Chawla Offset Printers, Delhi 110 052

CONTENTS

INTRODUCTION

The Song Of The Avadhut

Of all the mystical treatises of ancient Indian literature, the Avadhut Gita, or "Song Of The Avadhut," is one of the most eloquent and compelling. Its theme is the unitive knowledge obtained through mystical vision, the knowledge of the eternal Self. This knowledge is not limited to the mystics of any one cultural tradition, but is universal among all those who have attained to mystical vision. Men and women of all lands and all religious persuasions have experienced first-hand the eternal Reality, and realized It to be their own essential Identity. Some of the best known representatives of this universal knowledge are the Upanishadic rishis and Shankaracharya of the Vedantic tradition, al-Hallaj and Jalaluddin Rumi of the Sufi tradition, Shakyamuni and Ashvagosha of the Buddhist tradition, and Meister Eckhart and Juan de la Cruz of the Christian tradition. All have expressed the revealed knowledge of their identity with the one eternal Reality, and declared, in one way or another, their agreement with the words of the Christian saint, Catherine of Genoa, "My Me is God, nor do I recognize any other Me except my God Himself."

Throughout history, it has been the contention of the mystics of all cultural traditions that the "vision of

God" reveals man's essential oneness with Absolute Being, awakening him to his true, eternal Identity. Prior to such divine illumination, say these mystics, man suffers under the mistaken illusion that he is a limited and finite being, separate and distinct from other beings, who possesses his own individual identity. The dispelling of this illusion is called in different mystical traditions by different names, such as "enlightenment," "union with God," "liberation," "salvation," etc.; but it is, despite the various names, the same experience, the same knowledge that is revealed to all who have obtained the mystical vision.

Previous to the revelation of our absolute Identity, we live in confident certainty of our (illusory) individuality, regarding as "self" that kaliedoscope of transient mental impressions which is presented to our conscious awareness. But, say the mystics, this superficial play of thoughts, memories, sense impressions, upon the screen of awareness is but a mirage. It is the screen, the awareness itself, that is our true identity. It is that unchanging consciousness, the eternal witness of all movements of thought and appearance, which is who we really are. It is That which is our real, our only, Self.

The Song Of The Avadhut is one of the most sublime and uncompromising statements of this mystically perceived truth ever penned. Certainly, it is of Indian origin and is in the tradition of the

Upanishads, the Bhagavad Gita, the writings of Shankaracharya, and all those other scriptural treatises of India which may be classified as "Non-Dualistic Vedanta"; but it is an error to regard it as merely the expression of a particular philosophical school or religious faith. Its similitude to all those Non-Dualistic treatises preceding it is dependent, not upon a common learned tradition, but upon a common direct experience. The author of the Avadhut Gita was enlightened by the same direct revelation which inspired the Upanishads, the Bhagavad Gita, and other such works. It must be read, therefore, not as the reiteration of a conceptual position, or as an argument for the Vedantic viewpoint, but as the sharing by an illumined sage of directly revealed truth. His aim in this sharing is not to convince us, but to awaken us to the truth, and liberate us from error.

The Avadhut Gita is a call to knowledge, the supreme knowledge of ultimate Truth. The Avadhut holds out no compromise with illusion, he offers no foothold on separation, he allows no semblance of duality at all to creep into our perception of reality. Perhaps his knowledge is, for mere man, too sublime, too austere, too simplistic; but it is the knowledge of the ultimate, indisputable Truth of existence; and it is this very Truth which has the power to make us free.

The Author

The author of the Avadhut Gita was most certainly a Self-realized yogi and a master of Sanskrit verse; beyond that, we know very little. His Song has had many forerunners and many reaffirmations over the centuries; yet, of all the many such declarations of the knowledge of the one Self, none is more eloquent and compelling, none more convincing and illuminating, than this. Whoever the author of the Avadhut's Song might have been, there is no doubt that he was a great teacher, one truly established in the certainty of his supreme Identity. It is not only the profundity and genuineness of his vision, but the poetic beauty of his Song as well that has made it a source of joy and inspiration to his grateful readers over the years.

The author of the Avadhut Gita does not refer to himself by name, but at the end of each chapter, we are told that it was written by Sri Dattatreya. It is probable that this attribution is a later accretion, added to lend weight and credence to the utterances therein, and to insure their promulgation. The legendary Dattatreya of ancient mythology was said to have been an incarnation of Vishnu, born to the sage, Atri and his chaste wife, Anasuya; but as to whether such a person actually lived and what were the factual details of his life we know nothing at all. According to legend, he received the epithet of "Avadhut" when he renounced his royal heritage to become a wandering ascetic, living naked and free, far from the distractions of worldly men. The word, Avadhut, has become a generic term for all those homeless ascetics and yogis of India who live the life of total renunciation, unconcerned with the world and its "civilized" conventions, in order to remain concentrated on and identified with the eternal Self.

The actual date of authorship of the Avadhut Gita is unknown, but, judging by its terminology and style, it appears to have been written, not in the millennia prior to the Current Era, as legend would have it, but sometime around the 9th or 10th centuries of our Current Era. This does not, of course, preclude the possibility of an oral transmission to that point in time. Its theme is the same as that of the Upanishads, the Bhagavad Gita, and the writings of all illumined seers: the Self. It speaks, not of the soul or of God, but speaks rather from the experiential awareness in which that subject-object relationship no longer exists. It is a song of the final, ultimate, and irreducible Reality realized as I.

While his outlook is non-sectarian and iconoclastic, he frequently uses such terms as "Shiva," "Brahman," and "Purusha" to represent the absolute Self; but he uses these terms only to demonstrate their inadequacy. His intention is to demolish all sense of duality arising from the concept of a "God" separate from one's own Self, one's own essential Being. His outlook is identical, in fact, with that of the great Shankaracharya, who lived around the same period. Indeed, the Avadhut's Song is virtually indistinguishable from some of the writings of the illustrious acharya. Both sang of the need to recognize Brahman-Shiva-Purusha as the Atman, or Self; both asserted that the final spiritual attainment was identification with the Absolute, recognizing no other deity but the eternal I. Dualistic devotion might indeed lead one to knowledge of the Self, but from that point on, it becomes necessary to abandon all illusory dualities, and to become established in the awareness, aham brahmasmi ("I am Brahman") or shivoham ("I am Shiva").

To be sure, few men are capable of reaching such heights of knowledge, and fewer still are capable of sustained endurance in the rarified atmosphere at such altitudes of awareness. For this reason, a guide such as the Avadhut is most necessary and comforting to us. He leads us, confidently upward, over the rugged terrain of thought, and into the remote realms of unconditioned awareness. As we follow him into the dizzying heights of unitive knowledge, we are privileged to share in some measure his exalted state. Reading only a few verses of the Avadhut's Song, our minds are immediately lifted to a realm of immeasurable calm and certainty. A few more verses, and we've become immoveable, invincible, unruffled, secure once more in the recalled knowledge of our own eternal Self, which, somehow, we had forgotten. Thus, simply by reading the words of this master guide, we are lifted into the freedom and exultation of his pure awareness, and made capable of tasting a little of the sweet nectar of our own intrinsic bliss.

The Translation

The author of the Avadhut Gita expressed his thought in an extremely compacted form, utilizing several very brief and concise poetic metres. The meaning of the verses is therefore so condensed that the reader or translator is required, in many instances, to supply for himself the meat of the meaning to the bare bones which are provided. For this reason, a number of quite differently interpreted translations have been produced from the same Sanskrit text. In attempting a translation of this work, therefore, a certain familiarity with the thought of the Avadhut, and his state of awareness, is a greater asset than a purely linguistic competance.

I have attempted, in my own translation of this work, to adhere very closely to the literal meaning of the text, while at the same time taking certain liberties in order to bring out the full intent of the author's words. Moreover, I have assumed the burden of retaining as much as possible the poetic and rhythmic form of the original. My own translation is therefore also very compressed, requiring some additional elucidation of the text to be appended in the Notes. But I have aimed throughout to provide a readable English facsimile of the original, with as little dependence on extraneous notation as possible.

I have included the original transliterated Sanskrit on pages facing the English translation as a reference for the casual student of Sanskrit terminology; but even those with no familiarity with Sanskrit will find it interesting and facinating, I think, to read aloud the transliterated Sanskrit for its exquisite evenness of poetic rhythms and its hypnotic symphony of sounds. Even without a knowledge of their meaning, one can sense from a reading of these Sanskrit verses, the almost superhuman poetic genius of their author, and the powerful audial effect of the work as a whole.

— S. Abhayananda

The fool thinks, "I am the body." The intelligent man thinks, "I am an individual soul united with the body." But the wise man, in the greatness of his knowledge and spiritual discrimination, sees the Self as the only reality, and thinks, "I am Brahman."

— Sri Shankaracharya
Vivekachudamani

The Song of The Avadhut

AVADHUT GITA

Prathamodhyayah

1\.

ishvaranugrahad-eva
pumsam advaita vasana
mahadbhaya paritranat
vipranam upajayate

2\.

yenedam puritam sarvam
atmanaivatman atmani
nirakaram katham vande
hyabhinnam shivam avyayam

3\.

panchabhutatmakam vishvam
marichi-jala sannibham
kasyapyaho namas-kuryam
aham eko niranjanah

4\.

atmaiva kevalam sarvam
bhedabhedo na vidyate
asti nasti katham bruyam
vismayah pratibhati me

SONG OF THE AVADHUT

Chapter One

1.

Truly, it is by the grace of God
That the knowledge of Unity arises within.
Then a man is released at last
From the great fear of life and death.

2.

All that exists in this world of forms
Is nothing but the Self, and the Self alone.
How, then, shall the Infinite worship Itself?
Shiva is one undivided Whole!

3.

The five subtle elements that combine to compose
this world
Are as illusory as the water in a desert mirage;
To whom, then, shall I bow my head?
I, myself, am the stainless One!

4.

Truly, all this universe is only my Self;
It is neither divided nor undivided.
How can I even assert that it exists?
I can only view it with wonder and awe!

5.

vedanta-sara-sarvasvam
jnanam vijnanam eva cha
aham atma nirakarah
sarvavyapi swabhavatah

6.

yo vai sarvatmako devo
niskalo gaganopamah
swabhava-nirmalas shuddah
sa evaham na samshayah

7.

aham eva vyayonantah
shuddha-vijnana-vigrahah
sukham duhkham na janami
katham kasyapi vartate

8.

na manasam karma shubhashubham me
na kayikam karma shubhashubham me
na vachikam karma shubhashubham me
jnanamritam shuddham atindriyoham

5.

What, then, is the heart of the highest truth,
The core of knowledge, the wisdom supreme?
It is, "I am the Self, the formless One;
By my very nature, I am pervading all."

6.

That one God who shines within everything,
Who is formless like the cloudless sky,
Is the pure, stainless, Self of all.
Without any doubt, that is who I am.

7.

I'm the infinite and immutable One;
I'm pure Consciousness, without any form.
I don't know how, or to whom,
Joy and sorrow appear in this world.

8.

I have no mental karma, either good or bad;
I have no physical karma, either good or bad.
I have no verbal karma, either good or bad. [1]
I'm beyond the senses; I'm the pure nectar of the
knowledge of the Self.

9.

mano vai gaganakaram
mano vai sarvato mukham
manatitam manah sarvam
na manah paramarthatah

10.

aham ekam idam sarvam
vyomatitam nirantaram
pashyami katham atmanam
pratyaksham va tirohitam

11.

twam evam ekam hi katham na buddhyase
samam hi sarveshu vimrishtam avyayam
sadoditosi twam akhanditah prabho
diva cha naktam cho katham hi manyase

12.

atmanam satatam viddhi
sarvatraikam nirantaram
aham dhyata param dhyeyam
akhandam khandyale katham

9.

The mind is formless like the sky,
Yet it wears a million faces.
It appears as images from the past, or as worldly forms;
But it is not the supreme Self.

10.

I'm One; I'm all of this!
Yet I'm undifferentiated, beyond all forms.
How, then, do I regard the Self?
As both the Unmanifest and the manifest world.

11.

You, also, are the One! Why don't you understand?
You're the unchanging Self, the same within everyone.
You're truly illimitable; you're the all-pervading Light.
For you, how can there be any distinction between the day and the night? [2]

12.

Understand that the Self is continuous Being,
The One within all, without any division.
The "I" is both the subject and the supreme object of meditation;
How can you see two in That which is One?

13.

na jato no murtosi twam
na te dehah kadachana
sarvam brahmeti vikhyatam
braviti bahudha shrutih

14.

sa bahyabhyantarosi twam
shivah sarvatra sarvada
itas tatah katham bhrantah
pradhavasi pishachavat

15.

samyogash cha viyogash cho
vartate na cha te na me
na twam naham jagan nedam
sarvam atmaiva kevalam

16.

shabdadi panchakasyasya
naivasi twam na te punah
twam eva paramam tattvam
atah kim paritapyase

17.

janma murtyuh na te chittam
bandha mokshas shubhashubhau
katham rodishi re vatsa
nama rupam na te na me

13.

Neither birth nor death pertain to you;
You have never been a body.
It is well known that "All is Brahman";
The scriptures have stated this in various ways.

14.

You are That which is both inside and out;
You're Shiva; you're everything everywhere.
Why, then, are you so deluded?
Why do you run about like a frightened ghost?

15.

There's no such thing as union or separation for me
or for you.
There is no me, no you, no manifold world;
All is the Self, and the Self alone.

16.

You can't be heard, or smelled, or tasted;
You can't be seen, or sensed by touch.
Truly, you're the ultimate Reality;
Why, then, should you be troubled so?

17.

Neither birth, nor death, nor the active mind,
Nor bondage, nor liberation, affects you at all.
Why then, my dear, do you grieve in this way?
You and I have no name or form.

18.

aho chitta katham bhrantah
pradhavasi pishachavat
abhinnam pashya chatmanam
raga-tyagat sukhi bhava

19.

twam eva tattvam hi vikara-varjitam
niskampam ekam hi vimoksha-vigraham
na te cha rago hyatha va viragah
katham hi santapyasi kama-kamatah

20.

vadanti shrutayah sarvah
nirjunam shuddham avyayam
ashariram samam tattvam
tan mam viddhi na samshayah

21.

sakaram anritam viddhi
nirakaram nirantaram
etat tatvopadeshena
na punar-bhava sambhavah

18.

O mind, why are you so deluded?
Why do you run about like a frightened ghost?
Become aware of the indivisible Self!
Be rid of attachment; be happy and free!

19.

Truly, you're the unchanging Essence of everything;
You're the unmoving Unity; you're boundless
Freedom.
You have neither attachment nor aversion;
Why, then, do you worry and succumb to desire?

20.

All the scriptues unanimously declare
That the pure, formless, undifferentiated Reality
Is the Essence of all forms.
There is absolutely no doubt about this.

21.

All forms, understand, are only temporary
manifestations;
Only the formless Essence eternally exists.
Once this truth is realized,
There's no more necessity to be reborn.

22.

ekam eva samam tattvam
vadanti hi vipashchitah
raga-tyagat punah chittam
ekanekam na vidyate

23.

anatma-rupam cha katham samadhih
atma-swarupam cha katham samadhih
astiti nastiti katham samadhih
moksha-swarupam yadi sarvam ekam

24.

vishuddhosi samam tattvam
videhas twam ajovyayah
janamiha najanamit
yatmanam manyase katham

25.

tattvamasyadi vakyena
swatma hi pratipaditah
neti neti shrutir bruyat
anritam pancha-bhautikam

22.

The one Reality is ever the same;
This is what all the wise men say.
Whether you embrace or renounce desires,
The one Consciousness remains unaffected.

23.

If you see the world as other than the Self, can that be the experience of Unity?
If you see it as the Self, can that be the experience of Unity?
If it's seen as both the Self and not the Self, can that be the expeience of Unity?
The true state of freedom is to see everything as One.

24.

You are the pure Reality, always the same;
You have no body, no birth and no death.
How, then, can you say, "I know the Self"?
Or how can you say, "I don't know the Self"?

25.

The saying, "That thou art,"
Affirms the reality of your own true Self.
The saying, "Not this, not this,"
Denies the reality of the five composite elements. [3]

26.

atmanyevatmana sarvam
twaya purnam nirantaram
dhyata dhyanam na te chittam
nirlajjah dhyayate katham

27.

shivam na janami katham vadami
shivam na janami katham bhajami
aham shivash chet paramartha-tattvam
sama-swarupam gaganopamam cha

28.

aham tattvam samam tattvam
kalpana-hetu-varjitam
grahya-grahaka-hi-muktam
swasamvedham katham bhavet

29.

ananta-rupam na hi vastu kim chit
tattva-swarupam na hi vastu kim chit
atmaika-rupam paramartha-tattvam
na himsako vapi chachapyahimsa

30.

vishuddhosi samam tattvam
videham ajam avyayam
vibhramam katham atmarthe
vibhrantoham katham punah

26.

The Self is the identity of everyone;
You are everything, the unbroken Whole.
The thinker and the thought do not even exist!
O mind, how can you go on thinking so shamelessly!

27.

I do not know Shiva; how can I speak of Him?
I do not know Shiva; how can I worship Him?
I, myself, am Shiva, the primal Essence of all;
My nature, like the sky, remains ever the same.

28.

I am the Essence, the all-pervading Essence;
I have no form of my own.
I'm beyond the division of subject and object;
How could I possibly be an object to myself?

29.

There's no such thing as an infinite form;
The infinite Reality has no form of its own.
The one Self, the supreme Reality,
Neither creates, nor sustains, nor destroys anything.

30.

You are that pure and unchanging Essence;
You have no body, no birth, and no death.
For you, how could such a thing as delusion be?
How could delusion exist for the Self?

31.

ghate bhinne ghatakasham
sulinam bheda-varjitam
shivena manasa shuddho
na bhedah pratibhati me

32.

na ghato na ghatakasho
no jivo jiva-vigrahah
kevalam brahma samviddhi
vedya-vedaka-varjitam

33.

sarvatra sarvada sarvam
atmanam satatam dhruvam
sarvam shunyam ashunyam cha
tan mam viddhi na samshayah

34.

vedah na lokah na sura na yajnah
varnashramo naiva kulam na jatih
no dhuma-margo na cha dipti-margo
brahmaika-rupam paramartha-tattvam

31.

When a jar is broken, the space that was inside
Merges into the space outside.
In the same way, my mind has merged in God;
To me, there appears no duality.

32.

Truly, there's no jar, no space within;
There's no body and no soul encased.
Please understand; everything is Brahman.
There's no subject, no object, no separate parts.

33.

Everywhere, always, and in everything,
Know this: the Self alone exists.
Everything, both the Void and the manifested world,
Is nothing but my Self; of this I am certain.

34.

There are no divine scriptures, no world, no
imperative religious practices;
There are no gods, no classes or races of men,
No stages of life, no superior or inferior;
There's nothing but Brahman, the supreme Reality.

35.

vyapya-vyapaka-nirmuktam
twam ekah saphalam yadi
pratyaksham chaparoksam cha
atmanam manyase katham

36.

advaitam kecid icchanti
dvaitam icchanti chapare
samam tattvam na vindanti
dvaitadvaita-vivarjitam

37.

shvetadi-varna-rahitam
shabdadi-guna-varjitam
kathayanti katham tattvam
manovacham agocharam

38.

yadanritam idam sarvam
dehadi gaganopamam
tada hi brahma samvetti
na te dvaita-parampara

35.

The subject and object are unseparated and
inseparable;
That undivided One is you.
When this is so, when no "other" exists,
How could the Self be objectively perceived?

36.

Non-duality is taught by some;
Some others teach duality.
They don't understand that the all-pervading Reality
Is beyond both duality and non-duality.

37.

There is no color or sound to the one Reality;
It has no qualities at all.
How can one even think or speak of That
Which is far beyond both mind and speech?

38.

When you know all this universe of forms
To be as vacant as the sky,
Then you'll know Brahman;
Duality will forever cease to be.

39.

parena sahajatmapi
hyabhinnah pratibhati me
vyomakaram tathaivaikam
dhyata dhyanam katham bhavet

40.

yat karomi yad ashnami
yaj juhomi dadami yat
etat sarvam na me kim chit
vishuddhoham ajovyayah

41.

sarvam jagad viddhi nirakirtidam
sarvam jagad viddhi vikara-hinam
sarvam jagad viddhi vishuddha-deham
sarvam jagad viddhi shivaikarupam

42.

tattvam twam na hi sandhah
kim janamyathava punah
asamvedyam swasamvedyam
atmanam manyase katham

39.

To some, the Self appears as other;
To me, the Self is I.
Like undivided space, One alone exists.
How, then, could the subject and object of
meditation be two?

40.

Nothing of what I do or eat,
Or give or take,
Exists for me;
I'm Purity itself, beyond birth and death.

41.

Know that the whole of the universe is without any
form.
Know that the whole of the universe is forever
unchanging.
Know that the whole of the universe is unstained by
its contents.
Know that the whole of the universe is of the nature
of God.

42.

You are the ultimate Reality; have no doubt.
The Self is not something known by the mind;
The Self is the very one who knows!
How, then, could you think to know the Self?

43.

maya maya katham tata
chaya chaya navidyate
tattvam ekam idam sarvam
vyomakaram niranjanam

44.

adi-madhyanta-muktoham
na boddhoham kadachana
swabhava-nirmalas shuddhah
iti me nischita matih

45.

mahad-adi jagat sarvam
na kim chit pratibhati me
brahmaiva kevalam sarvam
katham varnashrama-sthitih

46.

janami sarvatha sarvam
eko tattva nirantaram
niralambam ashunyam cha
shunyam vyomadi-panchakam

43.

Maya? Maya? How could that be?
A shadow? A shadow? It doesn't exist.
The Reality is One; it's everything.
It's all-pervasive; nothing else exists. [4]

44.

I have no beginning, middle, or end;
I have never been, nor will ever be, bound.
My nature is stainless; I'm Purity itself.
This I know as a certainty.

45.

To me, neither the elemental particles
Nor the entire universe exists;
Brahman alone is everything.
Where, then, are the castes or the stages of life?

46.

I always recognize everything
As the one indivisible Reality.
That undivided One constitutes the world,
The Void, all space, and the five elements.

47.

na sando na puman na stri
na bodho naiva kalpana
sanando va niranandam
atmanam manyase katham

48.

sadanga yogan na tu naiva shuddham
mano-vinashan na tu naiva shuddham
gurupadeshan na tu naiva shuddham
swayam cha tattvam swayam eva buddham

49.

na hi panchatmako bhedo
videho vartate na hi
atmaiva kevalam sarvam
turiyam cha trayam katham

50.

na baddho naiva muktoham
na chaham brahmanah prithak
na karta na cha bhoktaham
vyapya-vyapaka-varjitah

47.

It's neither neuter, nor masculine, nor feminine.
It possesses neither intellect nor the power of thought.
How, then, can you imagine that the Self
Is either blissful or not blissful?

48.

The practice of yoga will not lead you to purity;
Silencing the mind will not lead you to purity;
The Guru's instructions will not lead you to purity;
That purity is your Essence. It's your very own Consciousness!

49.

Neither the gross body, consisting of five elements,
Nor the subtle body exists;
Everything is the Self alone.
How, then, could the fourth state or the other three states exist? [5]

50.

I am not bound, nor am I liberated;
I'm Brahman, and nothing else.
I'm not the doer, nor am I the enjoyer;
I do not pervade anything, nor am I pervaded.

51.

yatha jalam jale nyastam
salilam bheda-varjitam
prakritim purusham tadvad
abhinnam pratibhati me

52.

yadi nama na muktosi
na baddhosi kadachana
sakaram cha nirakaram
atmanam manyase katham

53.

janami te param rupam
pratyaksham gaganopamam
yatha param hi rupam yan
marichi-jala-sannibham

54.

na guruh nopadeshas cha
na chopadhir na me kriya
videham gaganam viddhi
vishuddhoham swabhavatah

51.

If water and water are mixed together,
There is no difference between one and the other.
It is the same with matter and spirit; [6]
This is very clear to me.

52.

If I've never been bound,
I can never be liberated.
How could you think that the Self—
With form or without—could be bound?

53.

I know the nature of the one supreme Being;
Like space, It extends everywhere.
And all the forms that appear within It
Are like the (illusory) water of a desert mirage.

54.

I have neither Guru nor initiation;
I have no discipline, and no duty to perform.
Understand that I'm the formless sky;
I'm the self-existent Purity.

55.

vishuddhosya shariro si
na te chittam parat param
aham chatma param tattvam
iti vaktum na lajjase

56.

katham rodishi re chitta
hyatmaivatmatmana bhava
piba vatsa kalatitam
advaitam paramamritam

57.

naiva bodho na chobodho
na bodhabodha eva cha
yasyedrisah sada bodhah
sa bodho nanyatha bhavet

58.

jnanam na tarko na samadhi yogo
na desha-kalau na gurupadeshah
swabhava-samvittir aham cha tattvam
akasha-kalpam sahajam dhruvam cha

55.

You are the one Purity! You have no body.
You are not the mind; you're the supreme Reality.
"I'm the Self, the supreme Reality!"
Say this without any hesitancy.

56.

Why do you weep, O mind? Why do you cry?
Take the attitude: "I am the Self!"
O dear one, go beyond the many!
Drink the supreme nectar of Unity!

57.

You do not possess intelligence, nor do you possess ignorance;
Nor do you possess a mixture of these two.
You are, yourself, Intelligence—
An Intelligence that never ceases, never strays.

58.

I'm not attained by knowledge, or samadhi, or yoga,
Or by the passage of time, or the Guru's instructions;
I'm Consciousness Itself, the ultimate Reality.
Like the sky, though I change, I am ever the same.

59.

na jatoham murto vapi
na me karma shubhashubham
vishuddham nirgunam brahma
bandho muktih katham mama

60.

yadi sarva-gato devah
sthirah purnah nirantarah
antaram hi na pashyami
sabahyantarah hi katham

61.

sphuratyeva jagat kirtsnam
akhandita-nirantaram
aho maya maha-moho
dvaitadvaita-vikalpana

62.

sakaram cha nirakaram
neti netiti sarvada
bhedabheda-vinirmukto
vartate kevalah shivah

59.

I have no birth, no death, and no duties;
I've never done anything, either good or bad.
I'm purely Brahman, beyond all qualities; [7]
How could either bondage or liberation exist for me?

60.

If God is all-pervading,
Immovable, whole, without any parts,
Then there is no division in Him at all.
How, then, could He be regarded as "within" or "without"?

61.

The whole universe is shining as One,
Without any split or break, or separate parts.
The idea of "Maya" is itself the great delusion;
Duality and Non-duality are merely concepts of the mind.

62.

The world of form and the formless Void:
Neither of these exists independently.
In the One, there is neither separation nor union;
Truly, there is nothing but Shiva alone.

63.

na te cha mata cha pita cha bandhuh
na te cha patni na sutas cha mitram
na pakshapato na vipakshapatah
katham hi santaptir iyam hi chitte

64.

diva naktam na te chittam
udayastamayau na hi
videhasya shariratvam
kalpayanti katham budhah

65.

na vibhaktam vibhaktam cha
nahi duhkha-sukhadi cha
na hi sarvam asarvam cha
viddhi chatmanam avyayam

66.

naham karta na bhokta cha
na me karma puradhuna
na me deho videho va
nirmameti mameti kim

63.

You have no mother, or father, or brother;
You have no wife, or son, or friend.
You have no attachments or non-attachments;
How, then, do you justify this anxiety of mind?

64.

O mind, there is neither the day (of manifestation)
nor the night (of dissolution);
My continuous Light neither rises nor sets.
How could a wise man sincerely believe
That the formless Existence is affected by forms?

65.

It is not undivided, nor is It divided;
It experiences neither sorrow nor joy.
It is not the universe, nor is It not the universe;
Understand that the Self is eternally One.

66.

I'm not the doer, nor am I the enjoyer;
I have no karma, either present or past. [8]
I have no body, nor are all these bodies mine.
What could be "mine" or "not-mine" to me?

67.

na me ragadiko dosho
duhkham dehadikam na me
atmanam viddhi mam ekam
vishalam gaganopamam

68.

sakhe manah kim bahu jalpitena
sakhe manah sarvam idam vitarkyam
yat sara-bhutam kathitam maya te
twam eva tattvam gaganopamosi

69.

yena kenapi bhavena
yatra kutra murta api
yoginah tatra liyante
ghatakasham ivambare

70.

tirthe chantyaja-hehe va
nashta-smurtir api tyajan
sama-kale tanum muktah
kaivalya-vyapako bhavet

67.

In me, there is no impurity such as attachment;
There is no bodily pain for me.
Understand that I'm the Self; I'm Unity.
I'm vast as space, like the sky above.

68.

O mind, my friend, what's the good of so much speaking?
O mind, my friend, all of this has been made quite clear.
I've told you what I know to be true;
You're the ultimate Reality. You're unbounded, like space.

69.

It doesn't matter where a yogi may die;
It doesn't matter how he may die.
He becomes absorbed in the Absolute,
As the space within a jar becomes absorbed (in the outer space when the jar is destroyed).

70.

Whether he dies near a holy river,
Or in an outcaste's hut,
Whether he is conscious or unconscious at his death,
He merges into Freedom, into Unity, alone.

71.

dharmartha-karma-mokshams cha
dvipadadi-characharam
manyante yoginah sarvam
marichi-jala-sannibham

72.

atitanagatam karma
vartamanam tathaiva cha
na karomi na bhunjami
iti me nishchala matih

73.

shunyagare samarasa-putah
tishthanekah sukham avadhutah
charati hi nagnah tyaktva garvam
vindati kevalam atmani sarvam

74.

tritaya turiyam nahi nahi yatra
vindati kevalam atmani tatra
dharmadharmo nahi nahi yatra
baddho muktah katham iha tatra

71.

All duties, wealth, enjoyments , liberation—
All people and objects in the world as well—
Everything, in the eyes of a yogi,
Is like the (illusory) water in a desert mirage.

72.

There is no action,
Either present, future, or past,
Which has been performed or enjoyed by me.
This I know, without any doubt.

73.

The Avadhut lives alone in an empty hut;
With a pure, even mind, he is always content.
He moves about, naked and free,
Aware that all this is only the Self.

74.

Where neither the third state (deep sleep) nor the
fourth state (samadhi) exists,
Where everything is experienced as the Self alone,
Where neither righteousness nor unrighteousness
exists,
Could bondage or liberation be living there?

75.

vindati vindati nahi nahi yatra
chando-laksanam nahi nahi tatra
samarasa-magno bhavita-putah
pralapitam etat param avadhutah

76.

sarva-shunyam ashunyam cha
satyasatyam na vidyate
ekatma swabhavah proktam
shastra-samvitti-purvakam

iti shri dattatreya virachitayam
avadhuta-gitayam atma-samvitti-
upadesho nama prathamodhyayah

75.

In that state where one knows nothing at all,
This versified knowledge does not even exist.
So, now,while I'm in the state of samarasa, [9]
I, the Avadhut, have spoken of the Truth.

76.

It is meaningless to differentiate between the Void and the world-appearance;
It's pointless to speak of "the Real" and "the unreal";
One Self, unchanging, exists alone.
This is what all the scriptures declare.

In this composition by Sri Dattatreya
Called The Song of The Avadhut, this is the First Chapter,
Entitled, "The Instruction On The Wisdom of The Self."

Dvitiyodhyayah

1.

balasya va sishaya-bhoga-ratasya vapi
murkhasya sevaka-janasya griha-sthitasya
etad-guroh kim api naiva vichintaniyam
ratnam katham tyajati kopyashuchau pratistham

2.

naivatra kavya-guna eva tu chintaniyo
grahyah param gunavata khalu sara eva
sindura chitra rahita bhuvi rupa-shunya
param na kim nayati naur iha gantu-kaman

3.

prayatnena vina yena
nishchalena chalachalam
grastam swabhavatah shantam
chaitanyam gaganopamam

4.

ayatnac chalayed yas tu
ekam eva chacharam
sarvagam tat katham bhinnam
advaitam vartate mama

Chapter Two

1.

You may be young, unlearned, and addicted to
pleasures;
You may be a servant or a householder; it doesn't
matter.
Does a jewel require a Guru in order to be
valuable?
Or is it worthless simply because it's covered with
mud?

2.

You may lack learning or literary skill;
You don't require such qualities as these.
Hold fast to the Truth, and let go of all else;
Even an unpainted boat will take you across.

3.

The Self appears as both
The animate and the inanimate world;
Yet It always remains in Its own peaceful state;
It is always pure Consciousness, as calm as the sky.

4.

Though appearing as the animate and inanimate
world,
The Self remains forever One.
Where, then, is the division?
There is no duality, it is clear to me.

5.

aham eva param yasmat
sarasarataram shivam
gamagama-vinirmuktam
nirvikalpam nirakulam

6.

sarvavayava-nirmuktam
tathaham tridasharchitam
sampurnatvan na grinhami
vibhagam tridashadikam

7.

parmadena na sandehah
kim karisyami vrittivan
utpadyante viliyante
budbudas cha yatha jale

8.

mahadadini bhutani
samapyaivam sadaiva hi
murdudravyeshu tikshneshu
gudeshu katukeshu cha

5.

Indeed, I am the highest Truth! I'm Shiva!
I contain the world, both subtle and gross.
I do not come, nor do I go.
I have no movement; I have no form.

6.

I'm unaffected by my component parts;
Therefore, though the gods may worship me,
In my perfect wholeness,
I recognize no distinctions such as gods.

7.

Neither doubt nor ignorance
Can cause the slightest ripple in me.
Let the modifications of the mind continue to occur;
They're merely bubbles rising to the surface of a
pond.

8.

The ephemeral elements that form all things
Manifest in many different ways:
Some things appear soft, others hard;
Some things appear sweet, and others sour.

9.

katutvam chaiva shaityatvam
murddutvam cha yatha jale
prakritih purushah tadvat
abhinnam pratibhati me

10.

sarvakhya-rahitam yad yat
sukshmat sukshmataram param
manobuddhindriyatitam
akalankam jagatpatim

11.

idrisham sahajam yatra
aham tatra katham bhave
twam evahi katham tatra
katham tatra characharam

12.

gaganopamam tu yat proktam
tad eva gaganopamam
chaitanyam dosha-hinam cha
sarvajnam purnam eva cha

9.

The qualities of clearness, coldness, and softness
Are but qualities of water.
Likewise, matter and spirit (prakriti and purusha)
Are but qualities of the one Existence.

10.

Beyond all speech, beyond all names,
Beyond the subtlest of all subtle things;
Beyond mind, intellect, and the five senses,
The stainless Lord of the universe remains ever One.

11.

If the universal Self becomes known,
How could "I" continue to be?
How could "you"
Or the sentient and insentient world still be?

12.

The Self is said to be like the sky.
Indeed, It is like the sky;
It's pure Consciousness, without any stain.
It is truly the all-embracing Whole.

13.

prithivyam charitam naiva
marutena cha vahitam
varina pihitam naiva
tejo-madhye vyavasthitam

14.

akasham tena samvyaptam
na tad vyaptam cha kenachit
sa bahyabhyantaram tishthat
yavacchinnam nirantaram

15.

suksmatvat tad adrishyatvat
nirgunatvach cha yogibhih
alambanadi yat proktam
kramad alambanam bhavet

16.

satatabhyasa-yuktas tu
niralambo yada bhavet
tal-layat-liyate nantar
gunadosha-vivarjitah

13.

It remains unaffected,
Though It takes the form of earth, air, water and fire.
Though It takes all these forms,
It remains always the same.

14.

All infinite space is pervaded by the Self,
But nothing else pervades the Self.
It is simultaneously within and without;
It cannot be limited or divided in parts.

15.

It's extremely subtle and cannot be seen;
It's primary to all qualities, the yogis say.
It is the state that underlies
All other temporary states of the mind.

16.

By practicing yoga unceasingly,
Without attachment to anything,
Little by little, a yogi is freed
From all effects of the qualities (gunas).

17.

visha-vishvasya raudrasya
moha-murcha-pradasya cha
ekam eva vinashaya
hyamogham sahajamritam

18.

bhava-gamyam nirakaram
sakaram drishti-gocharam
bhavabhava-vinirmuktam
antaralam tad uchyate

19.

bahya-bhavam bhaved vishvam
antah prakritir uchyate
antaradantaram jneyam
narikela-phalambuvat

20.

bhranti-jnanam sthitam bahyam
samyag jnanam cha madhyagam
madhyan madhyataram jneyam
narikela-phalambuvat

17.

Against the dreadful poison of worldly lust,
Which deludes men's minds,
There is only one antidote:
The nectarean awareness of the independent Self.

18.

The subtle images are seen within,
And the manifold forms are seen without;
But the independent Experiencer of both
Is known by all seers as the inner Self.

19.

Experienced without, It's the universe;
Experienced within, It's the power of life.
And deep within that inner life
The real milk-of-the-coconut resides.

20.

The outer knowledge is of the coconut's husk;
The subtler knoweldge is of the meat within.
And concealed within that subtle core
Is the coconut-milk of Consciousness—the Self.

21.

paurnamasyam yatha chandra
eka evatinirmalah
tena tat-sadrisham pashyet
bheda-drishtih viparyayah

22.

anenaiva prakarena
buddhi-bhedo na sarvagah
data cha dhiratam eti
giyate nama-kotibhih

23.

guru-prajna-prasadena
murkho va yadi panditah
yastu sambudhyate tattvam
virakto bhava-sagarat

24.

ragadvesha-vinirmuktah
sarvabhuta-hite ratah
dridha-bodhas cha dhiras cha
sa gacchet paramam padam

21.

On a full-moon night, the moon is seen
By unhazed eyes as one, alone.
The Reality should also be seen this way;
Where two are seen, that sight's impaired.

22.

Because there is one, and only one,
The mind which perceives two is false.
He who teaches this is truly great;
He deserves a thousand accolades.

23.

A Guru gives the gift of wisdom
To both the wise and the foolish man;
But only he crosses over this ocean (of life)
Who attains the knowledge of Truth for himself.

24.

He who is free from attachment, free from hate—
Engaged in securing the good of all,
Firm in knowledge and steady of mind—
Will reach at last to the highest state.

25.

ghate bhinne ghatakasha
akashe liyate yatha
dehabhave tatha yogi
swarupe paramatmani

26.

ukteyam karma-yuktanam
matir yantepi sa gatih
na chokta yoga-yuktanam
matir yantepi sa gatih

27.

ya gatih karma-yuktanam
sa cha vagindriyad vadet
yoginam ya gatih kvapi
hyakathya bhavatorjita

28.

evam jnatva twamum margam
yoginam naiva kalpitam
vikalpa-marjanam tesham
swayam siddhih pravartate

25.

The space inside a jar merges in the space outside
When the jar is destroyed;
The yogi, when the body's destroyed,
Merges into the universal Consciousness—his own true Self.

26.

The destiny of those devoted to action
Is the result of their thought at the end of their life;
But the destiny of a yogi established in Unity
Is not determined by his thought at the end.

27.

One may express in speech
The destiny of those devoted to actions,
But the destiny of those established in yoga
Cannot be told; they go beyond speech.

28.

A yogi has no particular path;
He simply renounces imagining things.
His mind then ceases of its own accord,
And the perfect state just naturally occurs.

29.

tirthe va antyaja gehe va
yatra kutra murtopi va
na yogi pashyate garbham
pare brahmani liyate

30.

sahajam ajam achintyam yas to pashyet swarupam
ghatati yadi yatheshtam libyate naiva dosaih
sakrid api tadabhavat karma kim chin na kuryat
tad api na cha vibaddah samyami va tapasvi

31.

nirmayam nispratimam nirakritim
nirashrayam nirvapusham nirashisam
nirdvandva nirmoham alupta-shaktkam
tam isham atmanamupaiti shashvatam

32.

vedo na kiksha na cha mundana-kriya
gurur na shishyo na cha yatra sampadah
mudradikam chapi na yatri bhasate
tam isham atmanam upaiti shashvatam

29.

Wherever a yogi may meet his end—
Whether beside a holy river or in an outcaste's hut—
His births are through;
He merges in Brahman.

30.

He who has realized the innate, unborn, incomprehensible Self
Never becomes stained while enjoying the fruits of his desires;
He remains always free of stain, free of karma.
The ascetic, concentrated on the Self, is never bound.

31.

He goes beyond illusion, beyond comparison, beyond form,
Beyond any support, beyond the body and its nourishment;
Beyond duality, fear, desire, and powers,
It's the Lord, the Self, the Eternal, he attains.

32.

His attainment is not the Vedas, nor initiation, nor a clean-shaven head;
It is not a Guru, or disciples, or bountiful treasures,
Or the practice of postures, or wearing of ashes;
It's the Lord, the Self, the Eternal, he attains.

33.

na shambhavam shaktika-manavam na va
pindam cha rupam cho padadikam na va
arambha-nispatti ghatadikam cha no
tam isam atmanam upaiti shashvatam

34.

yasya svarupat sacharacharam jagad
utpadyate tishthati liyatepi va
payo-vikarad iva phena-budbudas
tam isham atmanam upaiti shashvatam

35.

nasa-nirodho na cha drishtir asanam
bodhopyabodhopi na yatra bhasate
nadi-pracharopi na yatra kimchit
tam isham atmanam upaiti shashvatam

33.

He does not envision the form of the great Shiva,
or Shakti, or any other gods;
He does not see kundalini, or light-forms, or the feet
of God;
Nor does he perceive his own soul, like a jar with its
contents;
It's the Lord, the Self, the Eternal, he attains.

34.

That is the Essence from which the sentient and
insentient universe is born;
It is like the ocean which gives birth to the foam on
its surface.
It is That by which everything is maintained and
dissolved;
It's the Lord, the Self, the Eternal, he attains.

35.

His attainment is not breath-control, or fixed-stares,
or yogic-postures;
Nothing becomes learned or unlearned at all.
His attainment is not the purification of the nerves;
It's the Lord, the Self, the Eternal, he attains.

36.

nanatvam ekatvam ubhatvam anyata
anutva-dirghatva-mahatva-shunyata
manatva-meyatva-samatva-varjitam
tam isham atmanam upaiti shashvatam

37.

susamyami va yadi va na samyami
susangrahi va yadi va na sangrahi
niskarmako va sakarmakah
tam isham atmanam upaiti shashvatam

38.

mano na buddhih na shariram indriyam
tanmatra-bhutani na bhuta-panchakam
ahamkritis chapi viyat-swarupakam
tam isham atmanam upaiti shashvatam

39.

vidhau nirodhe paramatmatam gate
na yoginas chetasi bhedavarjite
shaucham na vashaucham alingabhavana
sarvam vidheyam yadiva nishidhyate

36.

He does not attain a "many" or a "One" that is
separate from himself;
It is not something other, like an object with length
and breadth.
It cannot be objectively proven, or compared with
anything;
It's the Lord, the Self, the Eternal, he attains.

37.

He may or may not attain concentration;
He may or may not attain freedom from the senses;
He may or may not abandon all actions;
It's the Lord, the Self, the Eternal, he attains.

38.

Beyond mind, intellect, body, and sense-organs;
Beyond the subtle elements, and the five gross
elements;
Beyond the sense of ego, and even the ethereal
body;
It's the Lord, the Self, the Eternal, he attains.

39.

Transcending all dictates, he abides in the Self;
His mind becomes free of the thought of duality.
Neither purity, nor impurity, nor distinctions of sex,
Nor fortune, nor misfortune, has any meaning for
him.

40.

mano vacho yatra nashaktam iritum
nunam katham tatra gurupadeshata
imam katham uktavato guroh tad
tad yuktasya tattvam hi samam pakashate

shri dattatreya virachitayam avadhuta-gitayam
atma-samvittyupadesho nama dvitiyodhyayah

40.

If the mind and speech can't reveal the Self,
How could the Guru's teachings reveal the Self?
How could a Guru reveal with words
That Essence of existence which is self-illuminating?

In this Song of The Avadhut composed by Shri Dattatreya,
In this "Instruction On The Wisdom of The Self,"
This is the Second Chapter.

Tritiyodhyayah

1.

guna-viguna-vighago vartate naiva kimchit
rati-virati-vihinam nirmalam nisprapancham
guna-viguna-vihinam vyapakam vishva-rupam
katham aham iha vande vyoma-rupam shivam vai

2.

shvetadi-varna-ratito niyatam shivas cha
karyam hi karanam idam hi param shivas cha
evam vikalparahitoham alam shivas cha
swatmanam atmani sumitra katham namami

3.

nirmula-mula-rahito hi sadoditoham
nirdhuma-dhuma-rahito hi sadoditoham
nirdipa-dipa-rahito hi sadoditoham
jnanamritam samarasam gaganopamoham

Chapter Three

1.

The distinction between "with qualities" and
"without qualities" does not exist in Him;
He's beyond both attachment and non-attachment;
Stainless, He's beyond all forms.
He's beyond both qualities and the absence ot
qualities; though formless, He's the substance of
all forms.
So how can I worship that Shiva, who exists
everywhere, like space!

2.

Shiva is not white or yellow; He has no color at all.
That supreme Shiva is both the cause and the effect.
Truly, I am beyond the process of thought; I'm Shiva.
Tell me, friend, how can I bow the Self unto the
Self?

3.

I'm neither beginningless nor with beginning; I'm a
Sun that never sets.
I'm neither concealed nor unconcealed; I'm a Sun
that never sets.
I'm neither illumined nor unillumined; I'm a Sun
that never sets.
I'm nectarean knowledge, unchanging bliss; I'm
everywhere, like space.

4.

niskama-kamam iha nama katham vadami
nissanga-sangam iha name katham vadami
nissara-sara-rahitam cha katham vadami
jnanamritam samarasam gaganopamoham

5.

advaita-rupam akhilam katham vadami
dvaita-swarupam akhilam hi katham vadami
nityam twanityam akhilam hi katham vadami
jnanamritam samarasam gaganopamoham

6.

asthulam hi no nahi krisham na gatagatam hi
adyanta-madhya-rahitam na paraparam hi
satyam vadami khalu vai paramartha-tattvam
jnanamritam samarasam gaganopamoham

4.

I'm desireless, with desire; how shall I speak of that?
I'm unattached, with attachment; how shall I speak of that?
I have no substance, and yet I have; what shall I say of that?
I'm nectarean knowledge, unchanging bliss; I'm everywhere, like space.

5.

I'm undivided, yet I'm every separate form; what shall I say of that?
I'm divided, yet I'm in everything; what shall I say of that?
I'm both eternal and non-eternal; what shall I say of that?
I'm nectarean knowledge, unchanging bliss; I'm everywhere, like space.

6.

I'm neither gross nor subtle; I neither come nor go.
I have no beginning, end, or middle; I'm neither great nor small.
I'm telling all the secrets of the supreme Reality:
I'm nectarean knowledge, unchanging bliss; I'm everywhere, like space.

7.

samviddhi sarva-karanani nabho-nibhani
samviddhi sarva-visayas cha nabho-nibhas cha
samviddhi chaikam amalam na hi bandha-muktam
jnanamritam samarasam gaganopamoham

8.

durbodha bodha-gahano na bhavami tata
durlakshya lakshya-gahano na bhavami tata
asanna-rupa-gahano na bhavami tata
jnanamritam samarasam gaganopamoham

9.

nishkarma-karma-dahano jvalano bhavami
nirduhkha-duhkha-dahano jvalano bhavami
nirdeha-deha-dahano jvalano bhavami
jnanamritam samarasam gaganopamoham

7.

Know well that all sense-organs are made of
emptiness;
Know well that all sense-objects are, likewise,
emptiness.
Know well that I'm the stainless One; I'm neither
bound nor free.
I'm nectarean knowledge, unchanging bliss; I'm
everywhere, like space.

8.

I'm beyond the intellect and inaccessible to the
intellect; it cannot reach to me.
I'm beyond vision, and inaccessible to vision; it
cannot reach to me.
I'm nectarean knowledge, unchanging bliss; I'm
everywhere, like space.

9.

I have no karma; I'm the sacrificial fire in which all
karma's consumed.
I have no sorrow; I'm the sacrificial fire in which all
sorrow's consumed.
I have no craving; I'm the sacrificial fire in which all
craving's consumed.
I'm nectarean knowledge, unchanging bliss; I'm
everywhere, like space.

10.

nishpapa-papa-dahano hi hutashanoham
nirdharma-dharma-dahano hi hutashanoham
nirbandha-bandha-dahano hi hutashanoham
jnanamritam samarasam gaganopamoham

11.

nirbhava-bhavarahito na bhavami vatsa
niryoga-yoga-rahito na bhavami vatsa
nishchitta-chitta-rahito na bhavami vatsa
jnanamritam samarasam gaganopamoham

12.

nirmoha-moha-padavita na me vikalpah
nishoka-shoka-padaviti na me vikalpah
nirlobha-lobha-padaviti na me vikalpah
jnanamritam samarasam gaganopamoham

10.

Sinless, I consume all sins; I'm the sacrificial fire.
Dutiless, I consume all duties; I'm the sacrificial fire.
Boundless, I consume all bondage; I'm the sacrificial fire.
I'm nectarean knowledge, unchanging bliss; I'm everywhere, like space.

11.

I'm beyond non-existence and beyond existence; these don't pertain to me.
I'm beyond both union and separation; these don't pertain to me.
I'm beyond both unconsciousness and consciousness; these don't pertain to me.
I'm nectarean knowledge, unchanging bliss; I'm everywhere, like space.

12.

I'm never swayed by attraction or repulsion; I never imagine these.
I'm never swayed by happiness or grief; I never imagine these.
I'm never swayed by passion or dispassion; I never imagine these.
I'm nectarean knowledge, unchanging bliss; I'm everywhere, like space.

13.

samsara-santati-lata na cha me kadachit
samtosa-santati-sukhe na cha me kadachit
ajnana-bandhanam idam na cha me kadachit
jnanamritam samarasam gaganopamoham

14.

samsara-santati-rajo na cha me vikarah
santapa-santati-tamo na cha me vikarah
satvam swadharma-janakam na cha me vikarah
jnanamritam samarasam gaganopamoham

15.

santapa-duhkha-janako na vidhi kadachit
santapa-yoga-janitam na manah kadachit
yasmad ahankritir iyam na cha me kadachit
jnanamritam samarasam gaganopamoham

13.

The clinging-vine of worldly existence cannot affect me at all.
Contentment and pleasures, however many, cannot affect me at all.
The bondage of ignorance—this world of appearance—cannot affect me at all.
I'm nectarean knowledge, unchanging bliss; I'm everywhere, like space.

14.

The worldly turmoil produced by rajo-guna has no affect on me.
The suffering produced by tamo-guna has no affect on me.
The pleasure of righteousness produced by sattva-guna has no affect on me.
I'm nectarean knowledge, unchanging bliss; I'm everywhere, like space.

15

Neither troubles, nor sorrows, nor pleasures have any affect on my intellect;
Nor can the difficulties attending yoga have any affect on my mind.
Whatever may happen to stir up the ego cannot affect me at all.
I'm nectarean knowledge, unchanging bliss; I'm everywhere, like space.

16.

nịshkampa-kampa-nidhanam na vikalpa-kalpam
svapna-prabodha-nidhanam na hitahitam hi
nissara-sara-nidhanam na characharam hi
jnanamritam samarasam gaganopamoham

17.

no vedya-vedakam idam na cha hetu-tarkyam
vachamagocharam idam na mano na buddhih
evam katham hi bhavatah kathayami tattvam
jnanamritam samarasam gaganopamoham

18.

nirbhinna-bhinna-rahitam paramartha-tattvam
antar bahir na hi katham paramartha-tattvam
prak sambhavam na cha ratam na hi vastu kimchit
jnanamritam samarasam gaganopamoham

16.

I've put an end to both wavering and unwavering;
I don't even imagine thought.
I've put an end to both dreaming and waking; I
neither sleep nor wake.
I've put an end to animate and inanimate; I'm
neither moving nor still.
I'm nectarean knowledge, unchanging bliss; I'm
everywhere, like space.

17.

I'm not the knower, nor something to be known; nor
am I the cause of knowledge.
I'm beyond the realm of speech, the mind and the
intellect;
How could the ultimate Reality ever be described by
words?
I'm nectarean knowledge, unchanging bliss; I'm
everywhere, like space.

18.

I'm beyond both division and non-division; I'm the
absolute Reality.
Within? Without? How could I be? I'm the absolute
Reality.
I was never created; I'm not an object with
substance.
I'm nectarean knowledge, unchanging bliss; I'm
everywhere, like space.

19.

ragadi-dosa-rahitam twaham eva tattvam
daivadi-dosa-rahitam twaham eva tattvam
samsara-shoka-rahitam twaham eva tattvam
jnanamritam samarasam gaganopamoham

20.

shana-trayam yadi cha neti katham turiyam
kala-trayam yadi cha neti katham disas cha
santam padam hi paramam paramartha-tattvam
jnanamritam samarasam gaganopamoham

21.

dirgho laghuh punar itiha na me vibhagah
vistara sankatam itiha na me vibhagah
konam hi vartulam itiha na me vibhagah
jnanamritam samarasam gaganopamoham

19.

I'm beyond the sorrows of attachment; I'm the one Reality.
I'm beyond the sorrows of destiny; I'm the one Reality.
I'm beyond the sorrows of worldly existence; I'm the one Reality.
I'm nectarean knowledge, unchanging bliss; I'm everywhere, like space.

20.

Since I am not the first three states of mind, how could I be the fourth (samadhi)?
Since I am not any of the three kinds of time, how could I be a fourth? [10]
I'm the root of serenity, the primal serenity; I'm the absolute Reality.
I'm nectarean knowledge, unchanging bliss; I'm everywhere, like space.

21.

Terms such as "long" or "short" do not apply to me.
Terms such as "broad" or "thin" do not apply to me.
Descriptions such as "angular" or "rotund" do not apply to me.
I'm nectarean knowledge, unchanging bliss; I'm everywhere, like space.

22.

mata pitadi tanayadi na me kadachit
jatam murtam na cha mano ne cha me kadachit
nirvyakulam sthiram idam paramartha-tattvam
jnanamritam samarasam gaganopamoham

23.

shuddham vishuddham avicharam ananta-rupam
nirlepa-lepam avicharam ananta-rupam
nishkhanda-khandam avicharam ananta-rupam
jnanamritam samarasam gaganopamoham

24.

brahmadayah sura-ganah katham atra santi
swargadayo vasatayah katham atra santi
yadyekarupam amalam paramartha-tattvam
jnanamritam samarasam gaganopamoham

22.

No mother, father, daughter, or son ever belonged
to me.
Neither birth, death, nor the mind ever belonged
to me.
I'm always unwavering, always steady; I'm the
absolute Reality.
I'm nectarean knowledge, unchanging bliss; I'm
everywhere, like space.

23.

My nature is boundless, beyond such distinctions as
pure and impure.
My nature is boundless, beyond such distinctions as
attached or unattached.
My nature is boundless, beyond such distinctions as
divided or undivided.
I'm nectarean knowledge, unchanging bliss; I'm
everywhere, like space.

24.

How could the god, Brahma, and all his attendants
live there?
How could the city of heaven, with all its people, live
there?
My only form is stainlessness; I'm the absolute
Reality.
I'm nectarean knowledge, unchanging bliss; I'm
everywhere, like space.

25.

nirneti neti vimalohi katham vadami
nisshesha shesha vimalohi katham vadami
nirlinga linga vimalohi katham vadami
jnanamritam samarasam gaganopamoham

26.

nishkarma-karma paramam satatam karomi
nissanga-sanga-rahitam paramam vinodam
nirdeha-deha-rahitam satatam vinodam
jnanamritam samarasam gaganopamoham

27.

maya-prapancha-rachana na cha me vikarah
kautilya-dambha-rachana na cha me vikarah
satyanriteti-rachana na cha me vikarah
jnanamritam samarasam gaganopamoham

25.

How may I speak of that stainless One who is both "this" and "not this"?
How may I speak of that stainless One who is the unsupported Support of all?
How may I speak of that stainless One who has no gender and yet has gender?
I'm nectarean knowledge, unchanging bliss; I'm everywhere, like space.

26.

I'm always the Supreme, whether I'm active or inactive.
I'm the highest bliss, beyond attachment and non-attachment.
I'm everlasting bliss, beyond both forms and formlessness.
I'm nectarean knowledge, unchanging bliss; I'm everywhere, like space.

27.

This Maya-dream of a world has no affect on me.
The crookedness and deceit of men has no affect on me.
The truth or falsehood of men's speech has no affect on me.
I'm nectarean knowledge, unchanging bliss; I'm everywhere, like space.

28.

sandhadi-kala-rahitam na cha me viyogah
hyantah-prabodha-rahitam badhiro na mukah
evam vikalpa-rahitam na cha bhava-shuddham
jnanamritam samarasam gaganopamoham

29.

nirnatha-natha-rahitam hi nirakulam vai
nischitta-chitta-vigatam hi nirakulam vai
samviddhi sarva-vigatam hi nirakulam vai
jnanamritam samarasam gaganopamoham

30.

kantara-mandiram idam hi katham vadami
samsiddha-samshayam idam hi katham vadami
evam nirantara-samam hi nirakulam vai
jnanamritam samarasam gaganopamoham

28.

I'm beyond the distinctions of night and day; I can't
be split in parts.
I never wake from within myself; I'm never
not-awake.
I'm never moved by thought at all; I never try to be
pure.
I'm nectarean knowledge, unchanging bliss; I'm
everywhere, like space.

29.

I'm neither "the Lord," nor am I "not the Lord"; I'm
the formless Self.
I'm beyond the presence or absence of the mind; I'm
the formless Self.
Know well that I'm free of everything; I'm the
formless Self.
I'm nectarean knowledge, unchanging bliss; I'm
everywhere, like space.

30.

I am a house that's empty; what may I say of that?
I do everything, and yet I do nothing; what may I say
of that?
I'm always in the even-state; I'm the formless Self.
I'm nectarean knowledge, unchanging bliss; I'm
everywhere, like space.

31.

nirjiva-jiva-rahitam satatam vibhati
nirbija-bija-rahitam satatam vibhati
nirvana-bandha-rahitam satatam vibhati
jnanamritam samarasam gaganopamoham

32.

sambhuti-varjitam idam satatam vibhati
samsara-varjitam idam satatam vibhati
samhara-varjitam idam satatam vibhati
jnanamritam samarasam gaganopamoham

33.

ullekhamatram api te na cha nama-rupam
nirbhinna-bhinnam api te na hi vastu kimchit
nirlajja-manasa karosi katham visadam
jnanamritam samarasam gaganopamoham

31.

I'm beyond being a soul or not a soul; I'm forever
shining forth.
I'm beyond being a cause or not a cause; I'm forever
shining forth.
I'm beyond both nirvana and bondage; I'm forever
shining forth.
I'm nectarean knowledge, unchanging bliss; I'm
everywhere, like space.

32.

Unlimited by a beginning, I'm forever shining forth.
Unlimited by the continuing play, I'm forever
shining forth.
Unlimited by the destruction of all, I'm forever
shining forth.
I'm nectarean knowledge, unchanging bliss; I'm
everywhere, like space.

33.

Though you may be spoken of, you have neither
name nor form.
Whether you are divided or undivided, there's
nothing here but you.
O mind, O shameless, wandering mind! Why do
you weary yourself so?
I'm nectarean knowledge, unchanging bliss; I'm
everywhere, like space.

34.

kim nama rodishi sakhe na jara na murtyuh
kim nama rodishi sakhe na cha jnama-duhkham
kim nama rodishi sakhe na cha te vikarah
jnanamritam samarasam gaganopamoham

35.

kim nama rodishi sakhe na cha te swarupam
kim nama rodishi sakhe na cha te virupam
kim nama rodishi sakhe na cha te vayamsi
jnanamritam samarasam gaganopamoham

36.

kim nama rodishi sakhe na cha te vayamsi
kim nama rodishi sakhe na cha te manamsi
kim nama rodishi sakhe na taventriyani
jnanamritam samarasam gaganopamoham

34.

Why do you weep and moan, my friend? There's no
old age or death for you.
Why do you weep and moan, my friend? There's no
pain of birth for you.
Why do you weep and moan, my friend? You can't
be touched at all.
I'm nectarean knowledge, unchanging bliss; I'm
everywhere, like space.

35.

Why do you weep and moan, my friend? You have
no form of your own.
Why do you weep and moan, my friend? You cannot
be deformed.
Why do you weep and moan, my friend? You can
never become old.
I'm nectarean knowledge, unchanging bliss; I'm
everywhere, like space.

36.

Why do you weep and moan, my friend? You can
never lose your youth.
Why do you weep and moan, my friend? You can
never lose your mind.
Why do you weep and moan, my friend? You have
no organs of sense.
I'm nectarean knowledge, unchanging bliss; I'm
everywhere, like space.

37.

kim nama rodishi sakhe na cha te sti kamah
kim nama rodishi sakhe na cha te pralobhah
kim nama rodishi sakhe na cha te vimohah
jnanamritam samarasam gaganopamoham

38.

aishvaryam icchasi katham na cha te dhanani
aishvaryam icchasi katham na cha te hi patni
aishvaryam icchasi katham na cha te mameti
jnanamritam samarasam gaganopamoham

39.

linga-prapancha-janusi na cha te na me cha
nirlajja-manasam idam cha vibhati bhinnam
nirbheda-bheda-rahitam na cha te na me cha
jnanamritam samarasam gaganopamoham

37.

Why do you weep and moan, my friend? You can't be touched by lust.
Why do you weep and moan, my friend? You can't be touched by greed.
Why do you weep and moan, my friend? You can't be touched by infatuation.
I'm nectarean knowledge, unchanging bliss; I'm everywhere, like space.

38.

How can you hanker after wealth? You have no property to support.
How can you hanker after wealth? You have no wife to feed.
How can you hanker after wealth? Nothing can be your own.
I'm nectarean knowledge, unchanging bliss; I'm everywhere, like space.

39.

You and I are not attached to this world of ephemeral forms;
It is only the shameless mind which divides the One in parts.
Division and non-division are the same to you and me;
I'm nectarean knowledge, unchanging bliss; I'm everywhere, like space.

40.

novanumatram api te hi viraga-rupam
novanumatram api te hi saraga-rupam
novanumatram api te hi sakama-rupam
jnanamritam samarasam gaganopamoham

41.

dhyata na te hi hridaye na cha te samadhih
dhyanam na te hi hridaye na bahih pradeshah
dhyayam na cheti hridaye na hi vastu-kalo
jnanamritam samarasam gaganopamoham

42.

yat sarabhutam akhilam kathitam maya te
na twam na me na mahato na guruh na shishyah
swacchanda-rupa-sahajam paramartha-tattvam
jnanamritam samarasam gaganopamoham

40.

Your nature does not contain even a little of dispassion;
Your nature does not contain even a little of passions either.
Your nature does not contain even a little of desire;
I'm nectarean knowledge, unchanging bliss; I'm everywhere, like space.

41.

There's no object of worship in your heart or in the state of samadhi;
There's no object of worship in your heart or in the objective world.
There's no object of worship in your heart; I'm beyond both place and time.
I'm nectarean knowledge, unchanging bliss; I'm everywhere, like space.

42.

I've told you all that constitutes the very core of Truth;
There's no you, no me, no superior being, no disciple, and no Guru.
The nature of the supreme Reality is self-evident and simple;
I'm nectarean knowledge, unchanging bliss; I'm everywhere, like space.

43.

katham iha paramartham tattvam ananda-rupam
katham iha paramartham naivam ananda-rupam
katham iha paramartham jnana-vijnana-rupam
yadi param aham ekam vartate vyoma-rupam

44.

dahana-pavana-hinam viddhi vijnanam ekam
avani-jala-vihinam viddhi vijnana-rupam
sama-gamana-vihinam viddhi vijnanam ekam
gaganam iva vishalam viddhi vijnanam ekam

45.

na shunya-rupam na vishunya-rupam
na shuddha-rupam na vishuddha-rupam
rupam-virupam na bhavami kimchit
swarupa-rupam paramartha tattvam

43.

How could the supreme Reality be of the nature of
bliss?
How could the supreme Reality be of the nature of
blisslessness?
How could the supreme Reality possess either
knowledge or ignorance?
If the supreme I am is the one Existence, It's
everywhere, like space.

44.

Understand that It's neither fire nor air;
Realize the One!
Understand that It's neither earth nor water;
Realize the One!
Understand that It neither comes nor goes;
Realize the One!
Understand that It's like space, pervading
everywhere; Realize the One!

45.

My nature is neither emptiness nor fullness.
My nature is neither pure nor impure.
I'm neither with form nor without form.
I'm the supreme Reality; my nature is uniquely
my own.

46.

muncha muncha hi samsaram
tyagam muncha hi sarvatha
tyagatyaga-visam shuddham
amritam sahajam dhruvam

iti shri dattatreya-virachitayam avadhuta-gitayam
atma-samvittyupadesha nama tritiyodhyayah

46.

Renounce, renounce the world of appearance;
Then renounce renunciation as well.
But, whether you renounce or do not renounce,
Enjoy the nectar of your natural state.

In this composition by Shri Dattatreya, called
The Song of The Avadhut,
In this Instruction On The Wisdom of The Self,
this is the Third Chapter.

Chaturthodhyayah

1.

navahanam naiva visarjanam va
puspani patrani katham bhavanti
dhyanani mantrani katham bhavanti
samasamam chaiva shivarchanam cha

2.

na kevalam bandha-vibandha-mukto
na kevalam shuddha-vishuddha-muktah
na kevalam yoga-viyoga-muktah
sa vai vimukto gaganopamoham

3.

sanjayate sarvam idam hi tathyam
sanjayate sarvam idam vitathyam
evam vikalpo mama naiva jatah
swarupa-nirvanam anamayoham

4.

na sanjanam chaiva niranjanam va
na chantaram vapi nirantaram va
antarvibhinnam na hi me vibhati
swarupa-nirvanam anamayoham

Chapter Four

1.

Where is the need to make offerings or prostrations?
Or to practice worship with flowers and leaves?
Why practice meditation and the repetition of
mantras?
The worshipper and Shiva are one and the same.

2.

I'm not only free of bondage and liberation;
I'm not only free of purity and impurity;
I'm not only free of union and separation;
I'm Freedom itself; I'm everywhere, like space.

3.

Some say, "The phenomenal world is real";
Others say, "The world is unreal."
Such arguments as these have no meaning to me;
My nature is Freedom; there's no maya to me.

4.

I have no faults, nor am I faultless.
I have no beginning, nor am I beginningless.
I'm not undivided, nor am I divided.
My nature is Freedom; there's no maya to me.

5.

abodha-bodho mama naiva jato
bodha-swarupam mama naiva jatam
nirbodha-bodham cha katham vadami
swarupa-nirvanam anamayoham

6.

na dharma-yukto na cha papa-yukto
na bandha yukto na cha moksha-yuktah
yuktam tvayuktam na cha me vibhati
swarupa-nirvanam anamayoham

7.

paraparam va na cha me kadachit
madhyastha-bhavo hi na chari-mitram
hitahitam chapi katham vadami
swarupa-nirvanam anamayoham

8.

nopasako naivam upasyarupam
na chopadesho na cha me kriya cha
samvit-swarupam cha katham vadami
swarupa-nirvanam anamayoham

5.

In me, ignorance and knowledge never arise;
I never allow myself to experience those states.
How, then, could I speak of not knowing or knowing?
My nature is Freedom; there's no maya to me.

6.

I'm not bound to righteousness; I'm not bound to sin.
I'm not bound to bondage, nor to liberation;
Neither of these affects me at all.
My nature is Freedom; there's no maya to me.

7.

"Inferior" and "superior" have no meaning to me.
I have no enemies, nor have I any friends;
How, then, could I speak of "the good" or "the evil"?
My nature is Freedom; there's no maya to me.

8.

I'm not the worshipper nor the object of worship.
I give no words of instruction, nor do I perform any actions.
My nature is Consciousness; how, then, could I speak?
My nature is Freedom; there's no maya to me.

9.

no vyapakam vyapyam ihasti kimchit
no chalayam vapi niralayam va
ashunya-shunyam cha katham vadami
swarupa-nirvanam anamayoham

10.

na grahako grahyakam eva kimchit
na karanam va mama naiva karyam
achintya-chintyam cha katham vadami
swarupa-nirvanam anamayoham

11.

na bhedakam vapi na chaiva bhedyam
na vedakam mama naiva vedyam
gatagatam tata katham vadami
swarupa-nirvanam anamayoham

12.

na chasti deho na cha me videho
buddhir mano me na hi chentriyani
rago viragas cha katham vadami
swarupa-nirvanam anamayoham

9.

There's nothing that pervades, and nothing that's
pervaded;
There is neither manifestation nor demanifestation.
How, then, could I speak of "the Void" or its
opposite?
My nature is Freedom; there's no maya to me.

10.

Truly, I am neither a perceiver nor an object of
perception;
I am not a cause, nor am I an effect.
How, then, shall I say that I'm "the knower" or
"the known"?
My nature is Freedom; there's no maya to me.

11.

There's no superimposer and nothing superimposed;
I am neither "the knower" nor "the object of
knowledge."
How, then, could I speak of creation or dissolution?
My nature is Freedom; there's no maya to me.

12.

I have no body, nor am I without bodies;
I have neither intellect, nor mind, nor senses.
How, then, could I speak of attraction or repulsion?
My nature is Freedom; there's no maya to me.

13.

ullekha-matram na hi bhinnam ucchaih
ullekha-matram na tirohitam vai
samasamam mitra katham vadami
swarupa-nirvanam anamayoham

14.

jitendriyoham tvajitendriyo va
na samyamo me niyamo na jatah
jayajayam mitra katham vadami
swarupa-nirvanam anamayoham

15.

amurta-murtih na cha me kadachit
adyanta-madhyam na cha me kadachit
balabalam mitra katham vadami
swarupa-nirvanam anamayoham

16.

murtamurtam vapi vishavisham cha
sanjayate tata na me kadachit
ashuddha-shuddham cha katham vadami
swarupa-nirvanam anamayoham

13.

One can't even speak of something separate from
the Self;
One cannot speak of what doesn't exist.
How, then, can I speak, friend, of "similar" or
"dissimilar"?
My nature is Freedom; there's no maya to me.

14.

I'm neither free of, nor bound by, the senses;
I follow no rules of "should" or "shouldn't."
How, then, can I speak, friend, of "success" or of
"failure"?
My nature is Freedom; there's no maya to me.

15.

I've never been either formless or with form;
I've never had a beginning, middle, or end.
How, then, can I speak, friend, of "youth" or of
"old-age"?
My nature is Freedom; there's no maya to me.

16.

I've never experienced death or deathlessness, nor
evil or good;
None of these opposites exist in me, my child.
How, then, can I speak of "impurity" or "purity"?
My nature is Freedom; there's no maya to me.

17.

swapnah-prabodho na cha yoga-mudra
naktam diva vapi na me kadachit
aturya-turyam cha katham vadami
swarupa-nirvanam anamayoham

18.

samviddhi mam sarva-visarva-muktam
maya-vimaya na cha me kadachit
sandhyadikam karma katham vadami
swarupa-nirvanam anamayoham

19.

samviddhi mam sarva-samdahi-yuktam
samviddhi mam lakshya-vilakshya muktam
yogam viyogam cha katham vadami
swarupa-nirvanam anamayoham

20.

murkhopi naham na cha panditoham
maunam vimaunam na cha me kadachit
tarkam vitarkam cha katham vadami
swarupa-nirvanam anamayoham

17.

I never experience sleeping, waking, or the deep
yogic trance;
To me, there is neither nightime nor day.
How, then, can I speak of the four states of the mind?
My nature is Freedom; there's no maya to me.

18.

Know well that I'm unaffected by the appearance or
disappearance of the world;
To me, there is neither maya nor its absence.
How, then, can I speak of the performance of right
actions?
My nature is Freedom; there's no maya to me.

19.

Know well that, in samadhi, all things are One;
Know also that I'm unaffected by the attainment or
non-attainment of samadhi.
How, then, can I speak of union or separation?
My nature is Freedom; there's no maya to me.

20.

I'm not unlearned, nor am I learned;
I don't remain silent, nor do I say anything.
How, then, can I speak of true or false doctrines?
My nature is Freedom; there's no maya to me.

21.

pita cha mata cha kulam na jatih
janmadi murtyur na cha me kadachit
sneham vimoham cha katham vadami
swarupa-nirvanam anamayoham

22.

astam gato naiva sadoditoham
tejo-vitejo na cha me kadachit
sandhyadikam karma katham vadami
swarupa-nirvanam anamayoham

23.

asamshayam viddhi nirakulam mam
asamshayam viddhi nirantaram mam
asamshayam viddhi niranjanam mam
swarupa-nirvanam anamayoham

24.

dhyanani sarvani parityajanti
shubhashubham karma parityajanti
tyagamurtam tata pibanti dhirah
swarupa-nirvanam anamayoham

21.

I have no father or mother; I have no family or caste;
I've never known birth, and I've never known death.
How, then, can I speak of affection or attachment?
My nature is Freedom; there's no maya to me.

22.

My awareness of the Self is constant; I never abandon it;
So I'm never affected by darkness or light.
How, then, can I speak of my morning or evening prayers?
My nature is Freedom; there's no maya to me.

23.

Know, without any doubt, that I'm limitless.
Know, without any doubt, that I'm changeless.
Know, without any doubt, that no stains can touch me.
My nature is Freedom; there's no maya to me.

24.

Those who possess strong determination renounce meditation;
They renounce all their good works as well as their bad.
The nectar of renunciation they drink to their fill.
My nature is Freedom; there's no maya to me.

25.

vindati vindati na hi na hi yatra
chando-lakshanam na hi na hi tatra
samarasa-magno bhavita-putah
pralapati tattvam param avadhutah

iti shri dattatreya-virachitayam avadhuta-gitayam
swami-kartika-samvade swatma-samvittyupadeshe
swarupa-nirnaya nama chaturthodhyayah

25.

In that state where one knows nothing at all,
This versified knowledge doesn't even exist.
So, now, while I'm in the state of samarasa,
I, the Avadhut, have spoken of the supreme Absolute.

In this composition by Shri Dattatreya, called The Song of The Avadhut,
In this dialogue between the Swami and Kartika, entitled The Instruction On The Wisdom of The Self,
This is the Fourth Chapter, called "The Declaration of My Nature."

Panchamodhyayah

1.

aum iti gaditam gagana-samam
tanna parapara-sara-vichara iti
avilasa-vilasa-nirakaranam
katham aksara-bindu-samuccharanam

2.

iti tat twam asi-prabhriti-shrutibhih
pratipaditam atmani tattvam asi
twam upadhi-vivarjita-sarva-sammam
kim u rodishi manasi sarva-samam

3.

atha urdhva-vivarjita-sarva-samam
bahirantara-varjita-sarva-samam
yadichaikavivarjita sarva-samam
kim u rodishi manasi sarva-samam

4.

nahi kalpita-kalpa-vichara iti
nahi karana-karya-vichara iti
pada-sandhi-vivarjita sarva-samam
kim u rodishi manasi sarva-samam

Chapter Five

1.

AUM pervades everything, equally, like space; [11]
Within It, there are no distinctions such as "high" and "low."
The formless Unmanifest manifests as form;
How else could the Imperishable show forth Its Light?

2.

"Thou art That," the scriptures proclaim;
"Thou art That," one's own Self affirms.
You are beyond all diversification, the same Self in all.
Why lament, then, O mind? I'm the same Self in all.

3.

Beyond "high" and "low," I'm the same Self in all.
Beyond "inner" and "outer," I'm the same Self in all.
If there is only the One, I'm the same Self in all;
Why lament, then, O mind? I'm the same Self in all.

4.

There's no real distinction between the Imaginer and the imagination;
There's no real distinction between the Cause and Its effect.
A poem and its words are one and the same;
Why lament, then, O mind? I'm the same Self in all.

5.

nahi bodha-vibodha-samadhir iti
nahi desha-videsha-samadhir iti
nahi kala-vikala-samadhir iti
kim u rodishi manasi sarva-samam

6.

nahi kumbha-nabho nahi kumbha iti
na hi jiva-vapuh na hi jiva iti
na hi karana-karya-vibhaga iti
kim u rodishi manasi sarva-samam

7.

iha sarva-nirantara-moksha-padam
laghy-dirgha-vichara-vihina iti
na hi vartula-kona-vibhaga iti
kim u rodishi manasi sarva-samam

8.

iha shunya-vishunya-vihina iti
iha shuddha-vishuddha vihina iti
iha sarva-visarva vihina iti
kim u rodishi manasi sarva-samam

5.

There's no knowledge and no ignorance in the experience of Unity;
There's no near and no far in the experience of Unity;
There's no time and no eternity in the experience of Unity;
Why lament, then, O mind? I'm the same Self in all.

6.

There's no space in the jar, nor even a jar;
There's no container of the soul, nor even a soul.
There's no separation between Cause and effect;
Why lament, then, O mind? I'm the same Self in all.

7.

Here, in the realm of Unity, everyone is eternally free;
A "short time" and a "long time" have no meaning here.
Here, no distinction such as "fat" or "thin" exists;
Why lament, then, O mind? I'm the same Self in all.

8.

Here is neither Emptiness nor fullness;
Here is neither purity nor impurity.
Here is neither the All nor its absence;
Why lament, then, O mind? I'm the same Self in all.

9.

nahi bhinna-vibhinna vichara iti
bahir-antara-sandhi vichara iti
ari-mitra-vivarjita sarva-samam
kim u rodishi manasi sarva-samam

10.

na hi shishya-vishishya swarupa iti
na charachara-bheda vichara iti
iha sarva-nirantara moksha-padam
kim u rodishi manasi sarva-samam

11.

nanu rupa-virupa vihina iti
nanu bhinna-vibhinna vihina iti
nanu sarga-visarga vihina iti.
kim u rodishi manasi sarva-samam

12.

na gunaguna-pasa nibandha iti
murta-jivana-karma-karomi katham
iti shuddha-niranjana sarva samam
kim u rodishi manasi sarva-samam

9.

There's no distinction such as "divided" or
"undivided";
There's no distinction such as "within" or "without";
Beyond the distinction of "enemy" or "friend," I'm
the same Self in all.
Why lament, then, O mind? I'm the same Self in all.

10.

There's no disciple or non-disciple in the one
Reality;
There's no one evolving, and no one not-evolving;
Here, in the state of Unity, everyone is eternally free.
Why lament, then, O mind? I'm the same Self in all.

11.

The Self is beyond form and formlessness, is It not?
It is beyond division and non-division, is It not?
It is beyond creation and the absense of creation,
is It not?
Why lament, then, O mind? I'm the same Self in all.

12.

Neither the gunas nor anything else can bind me;
How could I be bound by actions in this life or in the
after-life?
I'm the pure, stainless Self, the same within all;
Why lament, then, O mind? I'm the same Self in all.

13.

iha bhava-vibhava vihina iti
iha kama-vikama vihina iti
iha bodhatamam khalu moksha-samam
kim u rodishi manasi sarva-samam

14.

iha tattva-virantara tattvam iti
na hi sandhi-visandhi vihina iti
yadi sarva-vivarjita sarva-samam
kim u rodishi manasi sarva-samam

15.

aniketa-kuti parivara-samam
iha sanga-visanga vihina-param
iha bodha-vibodha vihina-param
kim u rodishi manasi sarva-samam

16.

avikara-vikaram asatyam iti
avilaksya-vilaksyam asatyam iti
yadi kevalam atmani satyam iti
kim u rodishi manasi sarva-samam

13.

Here is neither existence nor non-existence;
Here is neither desire nor desirelessness;
Here, the wisdom that's learned is freedom and equality;
Why lament, then, O mind? I'm the same Self in all.

14.

Here, Reality is not divided into sub-realities (tattvas);
Here is neither union nor separation.
Even if everything disappears, I'm the same Self in all;
Why lament, then, O mind? I'm the same Self in all.

15.

I'm not a vessel, a temple, a house, or a sheath;
Here, without association or dissociation, I am the supreme Reality.
Here, without knowledge or ignorance, I am the supreme Reality;
Why lament, then, O mind? I'm the same Self in all.

16.

Unchanging? Changing? Neither is the truth.
Purposeless? Purposeful? Neither is the truth.
If only the Self is perceived: that is the truth.
Why lament, then, O mind? I'm the same Self in all.

17.

iha sarva tamam khalu jiva iti
iha sarva-nirantara-jiva iti
iha kevala-nishchala-jiva iti
kim u rodishi manasi sarva-samam

18.

aviveka-vivekam abodha iti
avikalpa-vikalpam abodha iti
yadi chaikanirantara-bodha iti
kim u rodishi manasi sarva-samam

19.

na hi moksha-padam nahi bandha-padam
na hi punya-padam nahi papa-padam
na hi purna-padam nahi rikta-padam
kim u rodishi manasi sarva-samam

20.

yadi varna-vivarna vihina samam
yadi karana-karya vihina samam
yadi bheda-vibheda vihina samam
kim u rodishi manasi sarva-samam

17.

Here, everyone is the same conscious Soul;
Here, everyone is the one eternal Soul.
Here, only the one undivided Soul exists;
Why lament, then, O mind? I'm the same Self in all.

18.

Indiscrimination? Discrimination? This is ignorance.
Mindlessness? Mindfulness? This is ignorance.
If only the eternal One is seen: that is knowledge.
Why lament, then, O mind? I'm the same Self in all.

19.

There's no state of liberation and no state of
bondage;
There's no state of virtue, and no state of sin.
There's no state of perfection and no state of
imperfection;
Why lament, then, O mind? I'm the same Self in all.

20.

If I'm always the same, beyond caste and
castelessness;
If I'm always the same, beyond cause and effect;
If I'm always the same, beyond division and
non-division;
Why lament, then, O mind? I'm the same Self in all.

21.

iha sarva-nirantara sarva-chite
iha kevala-nishchala sarva-chite
dvipadadi vivarjita sarva-chite
kim u rodishi manasi sarva-samam

22.

yadi sarva nirantara sarva-gatam
yadi nirmala-nishchala sarva-gatam
dina-ratri vivarjita sarva-gatam
kim u rodishi manasi sarva-samam

23.

na hi bandha-vibandha samagamanam
na hi yoga-viyoga samagamanam
na hi tarka-vitarka samagamanam
kim u rodishi manasi sarva-samam

24.

iha kala-vikala nirakaranam
anu-matra krisanu-nirakaranam
na hi kevala-satya nirakaranam
kim u rodishi manasi sarva-samam

21.

Here, everything is eternal; everything is
Consciousness.
Here, only the Immutable exists; everything is
Consciousness.
Without any exception, everything is Consciousness.
Why lament, then, O mind? I'm the same Self in all.

22.

If everything is eternal, everything is myself.
If only the Stainless, the Immutable, exists,
everything is myself.
Whether daytime or nightime, everything is myself;
Why lament, then, O mind? I'm the same Self in all.

23.

I'm neither in bondage nor in freedom; I'm always
the same.
I'm neither united nor separated; I'm always the
same.
I possess neither knowledge nor ignorance; I'm
always the same.
Why lament, then, O mind? I'm the same Self in all.

24.

Here, time and timelessness cease to exist.
Here, atoms and particles cease to exist.
Only the absolute Reality never ceases to exist.
Why lament, then, O mind? I'm the same Self in all.

25.

iha deha-videha vihina iti
nanu swapna-susupti vihina-param
abhidhana vidhana vihina-param
kim u rodishi manasi sarva-samam

26.

gaganopama-shuddha vishala-samam
api sarva-vivarjita sarva-samam
gata-sara-visara vikara-samam
kim u rodishi manasi sarva-samam

27.

iha dharma-vidharma viraga taram
iha vastu-vivastu viraga taram
iha kama-vikama viraga taram
kim u rodishi manasi sarva-samam

28.

sukha-duhkha vivarjita sarva-samam
iha shoka-vishoka vihina-param
guru-shishya vivarjita tattva-param
kim u rodishi manasi sarva-samam

25.

Here is no difference between embodied and
bodiless;
To the Supreme, the subtle and gross states are
the same.
The Supreme is the same whether It's named or
unnamed;
Why lament, then, O mind? I'm the same Self in all.

26.

The one Purity, like space, is equally in all;
Transcending all forms, I'm the same Self in all.
Whether there are forms or no forms, the Essence
remains the same;
Why lament, then, O mind? I'm the same Self in all.

27.

Here, I'm unattracted to either virtue or vice;
Here, I'm unattracted to either form or formlessness.
Here, I'm unattracted to either dispassion or desire;
Why lament, then, O mind? I'm the same Self in all.

28.

Beyond pleasure and pain, I'm the same Self in all;
Here, neither sorrow nor gladness exists.
In the supreme Reality, there is neither Guru nor
disciple;
Why lament, then, O mind? I'm the same Self in all.

29.

na kilankura-sara-visara iti
na chalachala samya-visamyam iti
avichara-vichara vihinam iti
kim u rodishi manasi sarva-samam

30.

iha sara-samucchaya saram iti
kathitam nijabhava vibheda iti
visaye karanatvam asatyam iti
kim u rodishi manasi sarva-samam

31.

bahudha shrutayah pravadanti yato
viyadadir idam murga-toya-samam
yadi chaikanirantara sarva-samam
kim u rodishi manasi sarva-samam

32.

vindati vindati na hi na hi yatra
chando-lakshanam na hi na hi tatra
samarasa-magno bhavita-putah
pralapati tattvam param avadhutah

29.

The Self is neither substantial nor insubstantial;
It is neither identical, nor not identical, to the world.
It's beyond both enquiry and abstention from
enquiry;
Why lament, then, O mind? I'm the same Self in all.

30.

This [Self] is the underlying Essence of every
substance;
So how can you find distinctions in the one
Existence?
There is no object of perception outside of Itself;
Why lament, then, O mind? I'm the same Self in all.

31.

In many eloquent ways, the scriptures have said,
"This observable world's like a desert mirage."
If there's only the eternal One, I'm the same Self in
all;
Why lament, then, O mind? I'm the same Self in all.

32.

In that state where one knows nothing at all,
This versified knowledge does not even exist.
So, now, while I'm in the state of samarasa,
I, the Avadhut, have spoken of the supreme Absolute.

iti shri dattatreya virachitayam avadhuta-gitayam
swami-kartika samvade atma-samvittiyupadeshe
sama-drishti-kathanam nama panchamodhyayah

In this Song of The Avadhut, composed by Dattatreya,
In this discourse between Swami and Kartika,
entitled Instruction On The Wisdom of The Self,
This is the Fifth Chapter, called "Revelations of Equality."

Sastodhyayah

1.

bahudha shrutayah pravadanti vayam
viyadadir idam murga-toya samam
yadi chaika-nirantara-sarva-shivam
upameyam atho hyupama cha katham

2.

avibhakti-vibhakti vihina-param
nanu karya-vikarya vihina-param
yadi chaika-nirantara sarva-shivam
yajanam cha katham tapanam cha katham

3.

mana eva nirantara sarva-gatam
hyavishala-vishala vihina param
mana eva nirantara sarva-shivam
manasapi katham vachasa cha katham

4.

dina-ratri vibheda nirakaranam
uditanuditasya nirakaranam
yadi chaika-nirantara sarva-shivam
ravi-chandram asau jvalanash cha katham

Chapter Six

1.

In many eloquent ways the scriptures have said,
"This observable world's like a desert mirage."
If there's only the limitless One, all is Shiva;
How, then, and to what, could the Self be
compared?

2.

In the Supreme there is neither division nor
non-division;
In the Supreme there is neither activity nor inactivity.
If there's only the limitless One, all is Shiva;
What, then, is the need of austerities and rites?

3.

The one Mind is infinite; It pervades everything.
In the Supreme there is neither "without" nor
"within."
The one Mind is, indeed, limitless; all is Shiva.
How, then, could Shiva be defined in thought or in
speech?

4.

There's no distinction between day and night;
There's no distinction between dawn and dusk.
If there's only the limitless One, all is Shiva;
What's the difference if the Sun or the Moon shines?

5.

gata-kama-vikama vibheda iti
gata-cheshta-vicheshta vibheda iti
yadi chaika-nirantara sarva-shivam
bahir-antara bhinna-matis cha katham

6.

yadi sara-visara vihina iti
yadi shunya-vishunya vihina iti
yadi chaika-nirantara sarva-shivam
prathamam cha katham charamam cha katham

7.

yadi bheda-vibheda nirakaranam
yadi vedaka-vedya nirakaranam
yadi chaika-nirantara sarva-shivam
tritayam cha katham turiyam cha katham

8.

gaditaviditam na hi satyam iti
viditaviditam na hi satyam iti
yadi chaikanirantara sarva-shivam
vishayendriya buddhi manamsi katham

5.

It's beyond the duality of desire and desirelessness;
It's beyond the duality of action and non-action.
If there's only the limitless One, all is Shiva;
What, then, may be considered "without" or
"within"?

6.

If it's neither with substance nor without substance,
If It's neither a Void nor a non-Void,
If there's only the limitless One, all is Shiva;
How, then, could there be a beginning or an end?

7.

If there's no distinction between division and
non-division,
If there's no distinction between the knower and the
known,
If there's only the limitless One, all is Shiva;
What, then, is the third mental state, and what is the
fourth?

8.

What can be spoken of is not the Reality;
Neither what can be spoken of nor what cannot be
spoken of is the Reality.
If there is only the limitless One, all is Shiva;
How, then, can there be objects, or senses, the
intellect or the mind?

9.

gaganam pavano nahi satyam iti
dharani-dahano na hi satyam iti
yadi chaika-nirantara sarva-shivam
jaladash cha katham salilam cha katham

10.

yadi kalpita-loka nirakaranam
yadi kalpita-deva nirakaranam
yadi chaika-nirantara sarva-shivam
guna-dosha vichara matis cha katham

11.

maranamaranam hi nirakaranam
karanakaranam hi nirakaranam
yadi chaika-nirantara sarva-shivam
gamanagamanam hi katham vadati

12.

prakritih purusho na hi bheda iti
na hi karana-karya vibheda iti
yadi chaika-nirantara sarva-shivam
purushapurusham cha katham vadati

9.

Neither space nor air is the Reality;
Neither earth nor fire is the Reality.
If there's only the limitless One, all is Shiva;
Which, then, is the cloud and which is the rain? [12]

10.

If there's no distinction between a thought-image
and the world,
If there's no distinction between a thought-image
and the gods,
If there's only the limitless One, all is Shiva;
How, then, could there be a distinction between the
Real and the unreal?

11.

There's no distinction between the living and the
dead;
There's no distinction between alike and different.
If there's only the limitless One, all is Shiva;
How, then, could one speak of going or coming?

12.

There isn't any difference between Prakriti and
Purusha; [13]
There isn't any difference between Cause and effect.
If there's only the limitless One, all is Shiva;
How, then, could one speak of Purusha (the Self) or
not-Purusha?

13.

tritiyam na hi duhkha samagamanam
na gunad dvitiyasya samagamanam
yadi chaika-nirantara sarva-shivam
sthaviras cha yuva cha shishus cha katham

14.

nanu ashrama-varna vihina-param
nanu karana-kartir vihina-param
yadi chaika-nirantara sarva-shivam
avinashta-vinashta matis cha katham

15.

grasitagrasitam cha vitathyam iti
janitajanitam cha vitathyam iti
yadi chaika-nirantara sarva-shivam
avinashi vinashi katham hi bhavet

16.

purusha purushasya vinashtam iti
vanitavanitasya vinashtam iti
yadi chaika-nirantara sarva-shivam
avinoda-vinoda matis cha katham

13.

There is no childhood—the "third stage" of misery;
There is no infancy—the "second binding rope."
If there's only the limitless One, all is Shiva;
How, then, can there be old-age, infancy, or childhood?

14.

Is it not true that there are no life-stages or castes?
Is it not true that there are no causes or effects?
If there's only the limitless One, all is Shiva;
How, then, can one distinguish between the perishable and the Imperishable?

15.

It's futile to distinguish between the perishing and the Unperishing;
It's futile to distinguish between the created and the Uncreated.
If there's only the limitless One, all is Shiva;
How, then, can there be an Imperishable and a perishable?

16.

The "male principle" (Purusha) and his consort do not exist;
The "female principle" (Prakriti) and her consort do not exist.
If there's only the limitless One, all is Shiva;
How, then, could such a relationship exist?

17.

yadi moha-visada vihina paro
yadi samsaya-soka vihina parah
yadi chaika-nirantara sarva-shivam
aham eti mameti katham cha punah

18.

nanu dharma-vidharma vinasha iti
nanu bandha-vibandha vinasha iti
yadi chaika-nirantara sarva-shivam
iha duhkha-viduhkha matis cha katham

19.

na hi yajnika-yajna vibhaga iti
na hutashana-vastu vibhaga iti
yadi chaika-nirantara sarva-shivam
vada karma-phalani bhavanti katham

20.

nanu shoka-vishoka vimukta iti
nanu darpa-vidarpa vimukta iti
yadi chaika-nirantara sarva-shivam
nanu raga-viraga matis cha katham

17.

If neither desire nor repulsion exist within the female
principle,
If neither pleasure nor pain exist within the male
principle,
If there's only the limitless One, all is Shiva.
How, then, does this sense of "I" and "mine" arise?

18.

Neither righteousness nor unrighteousness exist; right?
Neither bondage nor liberation exist; right?
If there's only the limitless One, all is Shiva;
How, then, does the thought of sorrow or happiness
arise here?

19.

There is no distinction between the Giver and the
gift;
There is no distinction between the Receiver of the
sacrifice and the sacrifice.
If there's only the limitless One, all is Shiva.
How, then, could there be rewards for one's actions?

20.

The Self is free of both sorrow and pleasure, is It not?
The Self is free of both humility and pride, is It not?
If there's only the limitless One, all is Shiva;
How, then, does the thought of attachment or
non-attachment arise?

21.

na hi moha-vimoha vikara iti
na hi lobha-vilobha vikara iti
yadi chaika-nirantara sarva-shivam
hyaviveka-viveka matis cha katham

22.

twam aham na hi hanta kadachid api
kula-jati vicharam asatyam iti
aham eva shivah paramartha iti
abhivadanam atra karomi katham

23.

guru-shishya vichara vishirna iti
upadesha vichara vishirna iti
aham eva shivah paramartha iti
abhivadanam atra karomi katham

24.

na hi kalpita deha vibhaga iti
na hi kalpita loka vibhaga iti
aham eva shivah paramartha iti
abhivadanam atra karomi katham

21.

In the Self neither delusion nor non-delusion arises;
In the Self neither desire nor desirelessness arises.
If there's only the limitless One, all is Shiva;
How can you think there is such a thing as
indiscrimination or discrimination?

22.

Look, there's never even been a you or an I;
All talk about family or caste is untrue.
Truly, I'm Shiva, the one supreme Self;
How, then, should I worship? To whom should I
bow?

23.

The distinction between Guru and disciple proves
illusory;
The Guru's instruction proves illusory as well.
Truly, I'm Shiva, the one supreme Self;
How, then, should I worship? To whom should I
bow?

24.

The division between bodies is only imagined;
The division between places is only imagined.
Truly, I'm Shiva, the one supreme Self.
How, then, should I worship? To whom should I
bow?

25.

sarajo virajo na kadachid api
nanu nirmala-nishchala shuddha iti
aham eva shivah paramartha iti
abhivadanam atra karomi katham

26.

na hi deha-videha vikalpa iti
anritam cha ritam na hi satyam iti
aham eva shivah paramartha iti
abhivadanam atra karomi katham

27.

vindati vindati nahi nahi yatra
chando-lakshanam nahi nahi tatra
samarasa-magno bhavita-putah
pralapati tattvam param avadhutah

iti shri dattatreya virachitayam avadhutagitaya
swami-kartika samvade swatma-samvittyupadeshe
moksha-nirnavo nama sasto dhyayah

25.

There has never been any activity or rest;
The one Purity is stainless and motionless, is It not?
Truly, I'm Shiva, the one supreme Self;
How, then, should I worship? To whom should I bow?

26.

There is no distinction between "embodied" and "bodiless";
"Wrong action," "right action"—neither exists.
Truly, I'm Shiva, the one supreme Self;
How, then, should I worship? To whom should I bow?

27.

In that state where one knows nothing at all,
This versified knowledge doesn't even exist.
So, now, while I'm in the state of samarasa,
I, the Avadhut, have spoken of the supreme Absolute.

In this Song of The Avadhut, composed by Shri Dattatreya,
In this dialogue between Swami and Kartika, called Instruction On The Wisdom of The Self,
This is the Sixth Chapter, entitled "The Ascertainment of Liberation."

Saptamo adhyayah

1.

rathya-karpata virachita kanthah
punyapunya vivarjita panthah
shunyagare tishati nagno
shuddha niranjana samarasa magnah

2.

laksyalaksya vivarjita laksyo
yuktayukta vivarjita daksah
kevala tattva niranjana putah
vadavivadah katham avadhutah

3.

asha-pasha vibandhana muktah
shauchachara vivarjita yuktah
evam sarva vivarjita shantah
tattvam shuddha niranjanavantah

4.

katham iha deha-videha vicharah
katham iha raga-viraga vicharah
nirmala nischala gaganakaram
swayam iha tattvam sahajakaram

Chapter Seven

1.

A patched rag from the roadside serves as a shawl
To the Avadhut, who has no sense of pride or shame.
Naked, he sits in an empty shack,
Immersed in the pure, stainless bliss of the Self.

2.

His attainment is beyond attaining or non-attaining;
His state is beyond that of union or separation;
He's continually established in the one stainless
Reality.
How can the Avadhut either speak or not speak?

3.

Free from bondage to the fetters of hope,
Free from the yoke of acceptable conduct,
Free from everything, he's thus attained peace.
He is the stainless One, the pure Absolute.

4.

For him, where is the question of being embodied or
bodiless?
Where is the question of attachment or non-
attachment?
Pure and unpartitioned as the infinite sky,
He is, Himself, the Reality in Its natural form.

5.

katham iha tattvam vindati yatra
rupam arupam katham iha tatra
gaganakarah paramo yatra
vishayikaranam katham iha tatra

6.

gaganakara nirantara hamsah
tattva vishuddha niranjana hamsah
evam katham iha bhinna-vibhinnam
bandha-vibandha vikara vibhinnam

7.

kevala tattva nirantara sarvam
yoga-viyogau katham iha garvam
evam parama nirantara sarvam
evam katham iha sara-visaram

8.

kevala tattva niranjana sarvam
gaganakara nirantara shuddham
evam katham iha sanga-visangam
satyam katham iha ranga-virangam

5.

Where the Self is, how can there be any knowledge?
How can there be either forms or the absence of forms?
Where there is the Supreme, infinite as the sky,
How can there be any differentiation of objects?

6.

The Self is undifferentiated, like the formless sky;
The Self is the pure and stainless Reality.
For Him, how can there be difference or non-difference,
Bondage or liberation, division or change?

7.

There is but one Reality: the undifferentiated All.
How, then, could there be union, separation, or pride of attainment here?
He is the Supreme, the undifferentiated All;
Here, how could there be any substance or non-substance?

8.

Only the stainless, all-inclusive Reality exists;
It is a clear, pure, and continuous Sky.
Here, how could association or dissociation occur?
In the one Reality, how could there be any relationship or severance of relationship?

9.

yoga-viyogai rahito yogi
bhoga-vibhogaih rahito bhogi
evam charita hi mandam mandam
manasa kalpita sahajanandam

10.

bodha-vibodhaih satatam yukto
dvaitadvaitaih katham iha muktah
sahajo virajah katham iha yogi
shuddha niranjana samarasa bhogi

11.

bhagnabhagna vivarjita bhagno
lagnalagna vivarjita lagnah
evam katham iha sara-visarah
samarasa tattvam gaganakarah

9.

As a yogi, he is beyond union and separation;
As a bhogi (enjoyer), he is beyond enjoyment and non-enjoyment.
Thus, he wanders leisurely, leisurely,
While in his mind arises the natural bliss of the Self.

10.

How does one who is continuously bound here by knowledge and ignorance
Become free of both duality and non-duality?
How does a yogi here become natural and desireless?
By becoming aware that he's the stainless Purity, the enjoyer of unchanging bliss.

11.

The Destroyer is beyond destruction and non-destruction;
The Sustainer is beyond sustaining and non-sustaining. [14]
Indeed, how could substance or the dissolution of substance exist here?
The Reality is unchanging, like the formless sky.

12.

satatam sarva vivarjita yuktah
sarvam tattva vivarjita muktah
evam katham iha jivita maranam
dhyanadhyanaih katham iha karanam

13.

indrajalam idam sarvam
yatha maru-marichika
akhanditam anakara
vartate kevalah shivah

14.

dharmadau moksha paryantam
nirahah sarvatha vayam
katham raga-viragaish cha
kalpayanti vipashchitah

12.

Continuously united with, yet free from, everything,
The liberated are beyond all manifestation (tattvas).
Indeed, how could there be any birth or death here?
How can one here meditate on either forms or
formlessness?

13.

All this [world] is conjured by magic;
It's only the water of a desert mirage.
Beyond all differences, beyond all forms,
Truly, there is only Shiva alone.

14.

We're completely oblivious to everything—
From the performance of duties to the attainment of
liberation.
How, then, could those who profess wisdom imagine
That we possess either attachment or
non-attachment?

15.

vindati vindati na hi na hi yatra
chando-laksanam na hi na hi tatra
samarasa magno bhavita putah
pralapati tattvam param avadhutah

iti shri dattatreyavirachitayam avadhuta-gitayam
swami-kartika samvade swatma-samvittyupadeshe
saptamo adhyayah

∞ ∞ ∞

15.

In that state where one knows nothing at all,
This versified knowledge doesn't even exist.
So, now, while I'm in the state of samarasa,
I, the Avadhut, have spoken of the supreme Absolute

In this Song of The Avadhut, composed by Shri Dattatreya,
In this dialogue between Swami and Kartika, called Instruction On The Wisdom of The Self,
This is the Seventh Chapter.

∞ ∞ ∞

NOTES

1. I.8. Since Brahman, the Self, is forever beyond the activities of Maya, neither actions nor the results of actions (karma) may be said to affect the Self.

2. I.11. The words, "day" and "night" are used here to convey multiple meanings: they may signify the day of universal manifestation and the night of dissolution; or simply the diurnal alternation of daylight and darkness. The Avadhut makes the point that these alternations do not affect Brahman; the Self is always, one, always the same, regardless of the appearance or disappearance of the world.

3. I.25. In the Vedantic scriptures, the phrase, Tat tvam asi ("That thou art"), refers to Brahman, the Absolute. The equally oft-used phrase, neti neti ("Not this, not this"), refers to the world of appearance (Maya), made up, according to Vedantic cosmology, of the five basic elements: fire, water, earth, air, and aether.

4. I.43. The author denies the existence of any fundamental reality other than the Absolute, Brahman. Maya, while it appears to exist, does

not. There is no second, no accompanying shadow, attached to Brahman. It is Brahman, Itself, which appears as the world; and while Maya is a term used to signify the world-appearance, it must not be accorded an independent status as a reality in itself, in addition to Brahman.

5. I.49 The various states of consciousness according to traditional Vedantic psychology, take place in the four interrelated bodies: waking consciousness in the gross body, dreaming in the subtle (astral) body, deep sleep in the causal body, and samadhi in the supra-causal body. Since all these bodies are the products of Maya, which is but appearance, the four states of consciousness are also merely illusory possessing no eternal reality.

6. I.51. Prakriti and Purusha are synonymous with Maya and Brahman, or Shakti and Shiva. Prakriti is but the manifested appearance of Purusha; they are therefore the same, like water and ice. Matter is but the appearance of Spirit; the distinction between them is ultimately illusory.

7. I.59 Maya, the world-appearance, consists, according to Vedantic tradition, of three modes of the same energy, by which it brings about the

manifestation of all forms. These are the gunas, or "strands" which make up the entire fabric of nature. One is a positive, or active, mode of energy, called rajas; another is a negative, or inhibiting, mode of energy, called tamas; and the third is a neutral or balancing, mode of energy, called sattva. These are the three energy-modes of Maya; but Brahman, i.e., the Self, is entirely unaffected by the play of these gunas. It is nirguna, beyond the gunas.

8. I.66. See Note 1.

9. I.75. "In that state where one knows nothing at all" refers to that awareness of the Self in which all mental activity has ceased. Obviously, the author could not have written this Song in that state of awareness; but now, as he says, he is in the state of samarasa (literally, "same taste"), a peripheral state of equilibrium in which he retains the awareness of the Self, while mentally perceptive of the world as his own manifestation. It is while in this state that he has written this Song.

10. III.20. "The three kinds of time" refers to past, present, and future. Brahman is entirely beyond space and time, and may not be regarded, therefore, as existing in any kind of time.

11. V.1. AUM is said to be the primeval sound (the Word, or Logos), and is synonymous with Maya, Brahman's creative Power of manifestation. AUM, like Maya, is therefore ultimately identical with Brahman, and has no existence independent of Brahman.

12. VI.9 The "cloud" and the "rain" are used here as metaphors to represent the artificial division between the Creator and the created, between Brahman and Maya, Shiva and Shakti, the Eternal and Its appearance.

13. VI.12. See Note 5.

14. VII.11. Brahman, the Absolute, is traditionally represented as having three aspects: The Creator (Brahma), the Sustainer (Vishnu), and the Destroyer (Shiva). This refers to the cyclic appearance, sustained life, and disappearance of the phenomenal universe. But, says the Avadhut, all these abstractions are only Brahman; and since nothing other than Brahman Itself exists, nothing is actually created, nothing destroyed.

About The Translator

Swami Abhayananda was born Stan Trout in Indianapolis, Indiana on August 14, 1938. After service in the Navy, he settled in northern California, where he pursued his studies in philosophy and literature. In June of 1966 he became acquainted with the philosophy of mysticism, and experienced a strong desire to realize God. Abandoning all other pursuits, he retired to a solitary life in a secluded cabin in the mountain forests near Santa Cruz, California; and, in November of that same year became enlightened by the grace of God.

He spent four more years in his isolated cabin, and subsequently met Swami Muktananda who visited Santa Cruz in 1970. Shortly thereafter, he joined Muktananda in India, as his disciple; and later lived and worked in Muktananda's Oakland, California ashram, where, in 1977, he translated The Song of The Avadhut. In May of 1978, he returned to India and was initiated by his master into the ancient Saraswati order of monks, and was given the monastic name of Swami Abhayananda, "the bliss of fearlessness."

For the next few years he taught meditation in various cities throughout the U.S., but in 1981, unwilling to condone what he saw as abuses of power, Abhayananda left Muktananda's organization, and went into retreat once again, this time for seven years, in upstate New York, where he wrote a number of other books. At present, Swami Abhayananda resides in the Olympia area of western Washington state, where he continues to teach, write, and publish his works on the knowledge of the Self.